REMINDER TO SELF

REMINDER TO SELF

The Eight Life Principles for Living from Your Truest Self

MARLON HARTLEY LINDSAY

© 2008 EOTO Book Company, a Division of EOTO Publishing, LLC

All rights reserved. No part of this publication may be reproduced, stored in a retrieval system, or transmitted, in any form or by any means, electronic, mechanical, photocopying, recording, or otherwise, without the prior written permission of the author.

The author has made every effort to locate sources for reproduced material, but welcomes any information to further confirm these sources.

ISBN 978-0-9817624-0-1
First Printing

Editors: Green Onion Publishing, Catherine Leek, and Zebra Communications, Bobbie Christmas
Interior Design and Formatting: WeMakeBooks.ca, Kim Monteforte
Cover Design: Sherman Studios, Fran Sherman

EOTO Book Company
P.O. Box 370097
West Hartford, CT
06137-0097

This book is dedicated to my wife Amanda
for dancing to the jazz of my life as I play my music.

Foreword

Socrates is to have said, "A life unexamined is not worth living." While this may sound like a very harsh statement, it makes the point that to be alive and not live consciously is a tragedy. Living unconsciously is simply accepting the trance of a particular environment in which we are born. To be awake requires courage to examine ourselves in relationship to all contexts of our life. People are born to learn and to grow, to push against the boundaries of the old and create the new.

Socrates believed that as human beings we are the product of an intelligent universe, and as such must have the intelligence of the universe within us. It is believed that one can discover that intelligence within by asking the question and seeking the answer. We are living at a time where a vast amount of information is available to us at our fingertips and it is instantaneous. This information is about all sorts of topics and subjects including your physiology, your psychology, your sociology, and to a lesser degree your spirituality, however you may define that. But there is nowhere you will find information about the unique entity you call "yourself."

Morris L. West in his book, *The Shoes of the Fisherman*, says, "It costs so much to be a full human being that there are very few who have the enlightenment, or the courage, to pay the price... One has to abandon altogether the search for security, and reach out to the risk of living with both arms. One has to embrace the world like a lover. One has to accept pain as a condition of existence. One has to count doubt and darkness as the cost of knowing. One needs a will stubborn in conflict, but apt always to total acceptance of every consequence of living and dying."

We as human beings seem to have an innate curiosity about our existence. The curiosity creates many questions about our existence, our purpose and what meaning we may put on that existence. It seems we all have a wisdom within us, quite possibly the wisdom of the universe. It may be possible that we can access that wisdom by asking the right question and learning the skill of hearing the answer. It takes great courage to have an honest dialogue with yourself. It takes great courage to look into your heart and mind and face whatever you may find there. Because we can be conscious of our self, it is possible that we can learn from ourselves.

From Khalil Gibran we read, "The Teacher who walks in the shadow of the temple, among his followers, gives not of his wisdom, but rather of his faith and lovingness. If he is indeed wise, he does not bid you enter the house of his wisdom, but rather leads you to the threshold of your own mind." *(The Prophet)*

Like the Teacher we should approach the self with loving kindness of all that we may find there. Remember the greatest Teacher is always the best student.

As you read this dialogue, please reflect on your own answers to your own questions.

Enjoy and blessings,
C. Bradford Chappell, PhD

Acknowledgements

I am grateful for Catherine Leek. Not only is she a great editor but she is a gift from God. She took me under her wings and gently walked me through the process and the many steps of getting this book to you. Bobbie Christmas performed the first edits on this work and showed me the fundamentals of writing.

My greatest appreciation goes to my wife for telling me to simply write when I doubted myself. I am thankful to my mother for her quirky but undying belief in me. I am in love with my three little girls Skye, Makenna, and Bliss.

I am grateful to Brad and Flora Chappell for their love and full embrace. Claire Lindsay, you are my father's better half and I thank you for your kindness over the years. We come into this life to experience the fullness of it, to gain strength, develop courage, and to experience gratitude. The essence of gratitude is expecting nothing and being thankful for everything. I am truly grateful to my fathers, Albert and Sam, for the experiences they gave me. I am nostalgic about my life in Jamaica, in particular Seven Miles and Harbour View, where my cousins taught me how not to be an only child at the behest of my grandmother Iris Taylor whom I miss the most.

I have learned many things through Da Fellas: Collin Robinson, Joe Samuel, Mike Christie, Tony DePass, Dave Daniels, Delroy Thomas, Hugh Ryan, Campbell (Bert) Singleton, Rohan Freeman, and Reggie Isaacs. Eurel Tobias would have been a part of the group but while we went to UCONN, he went to Columbia. Still, where I matured with Da Fellas, Eurel and I squeezed every ounce out of life—at least we tried.

I ventured into business with Tom and Laurie. We learned a lot, got a lickin' but we're still tickin'. I met Erin Reynolds, and Carl and Shirley Dudley, angels on the path. Siobhan Becker is remarkable. She has taken an idea of serving first-time homebuyers and breathed life into a great product—the *First-Time Home Buyer Magazine*. I reached the summit of Mount Galena together and in spirit with Wally Barnes, Bruce Douglas, Rita Rivera, Peggy Sayers, Michael Maglio, John Bailey, Patsy Darity, Maureen Muganda, Jim Muntz, Maura Melly, and Jessie Stratton. I cherish that memory. Joel Lavenson and I are gonna save the world one day, or at least take 'em to Maine.

Finally I have become because they were. Many spiritual trajectories on one journey. I can't remember how I was introduced to him, but Wayne Dyer taught me the most. I met Deepak before I met Wayne. I have

ACKNOWLEDGEMENTS

had long, endless conversations about God with Fred and Jan March, my treasured friends. Jim Rinere talking to you is fresh air. Carol Biancardi introduced me to Dan Millman. Mike Wilbur made me cry. Tonya Anderson sent me Caroline Myss. Amy Couch caused me to listen and linked me to the Omega Institute. Omega introduced me to Debbie Ford. I met Rita Woodard through Debbie Ford. I have done the most with, through, and because of Debbie—she introduced me to Amanda, who I married. Whew! Marrying Amanda was a package deal as I gained access to the wisdom of her dad, C. Brad Chappell. Brad is big on Kahlil Gibran. Greg Sears introduced me to Neale Donald Walsh. Amy Sailor thought I should read Eckhart Tolle. Earl Nightingale filled the role of an old wise grandfather. Earl Stone made me look like a basketball coach but he did the work. Jim Heidenreich is the genius who sprinkled some fairy dust on the websites and made them simple—simple is not always easy.

I have learned the most about families through the Church of Jesus Christ of Latter Day Saints.

I am forever grateful to all of you who are here and those who I have left out. I stand on your shoulders.

Preface

This book is a dialogue with myself. It is an ongoing dialogue that has changed as I have grown with the years, mentally and spiritually. The nature of the dialogue transformed as I was headed for a significant shift in my life. A life-change, more like a vicissitude, arose that gave me time to explore a more focused dialogue that resulted in a way of being, that held a greater meaning to life.

I lost everything, almost.

I was no longer invincible and life humbled me. I was humbled before God, I was humbled before my wife—I was a newlywed—and I was humbled before my friends and family.

There was no need to reflect on what went wrong; I knew, you know when your life is not right. *Reminder to Self* is a divine intervention that was to pull me from the onset of a deep, dark depression. I got clear instructions on how to be, how to walk into life, and how to live it fully, in truth, in light, and in God. So I began to talk to myself and I began to listen. It has made all the difference.

I now know that the reminders weren't just for me; I was given something to share, and with it a connection to my purpose. *Reminder To Self* is a self-evident way of being that promises to fill the void and light the way to a fulfilled life.

I share this seemingly odd experience with you to validate or encourage your own internal dialogue, so that your adventure may be deliberate, mindful, and connected to the one purpose.

I hope that after you read this book you will recognize that greatness is ignorant of origins. Use your endowments—power, knowledge, wisdom, light, and truth—as you connect to your truest self and your purpose. As you find your way, you will be taken to places unimaginable.

Thank you for your company on this amazing journey.

Table of Contents

My Story: Divine Intervention 1

The Wisdom of God is Within You 9

Chapter 1: Practice Self-love 31
Chapter 2: Be Deliberate with Your Choices 47
Chapter 3: Be in the Moment 67
Chapter 4: Live with Integrity 83
Chapter 5: Live in Abundance 95
Chapter 6: Detach from Your Outcomes 109
Chapter 7: Open Up Your Heart 123
Chapter 8: Live Today in Joy 137

The Beginning: Smelling Roses 147

My Story: Divine Intervention

My life was going well, or at least as well as it could be under the circumstances. I had a company that I started with two partners and I was finally starting to see the folly in our union—thinking, planning, and execution. Basically the partnership had run its course. Not every relationship is meant to last a lifetime. My life seemed to be about people dancing in and out of it, leaving opportunities for me to gain perspective that prepared me to experience myself outside of my areas of comfort.

We are socialized to hoard everything, including relationships, but holding onto a relationship for too long is like over-watering a plant; eventually it rots from the root. It was time to repot myself and we dissolved the partnership. It wasn't pretty.

I lost almost everything—my family was rock-solid, quirky, but solid. The rest of my life was built on sand. It was unsettling to know that my life was a mirage. I had to step out of the illusion to realize I was in it and when I did, it made all the difference.

I had graduated from university some 15 years earlier. Keen to make my place in the world, I immediately jumped into the workforce and put aside my desire to backpack through Europe—the modern-day version of the "classical tour". After moving very quickly, life slowed to a crawl, forcing me into early introspection, like early retirement except I was retiring from a way of being that no longer satisfied my soul, and there was no spiritual pension. My introspection was not an ordinary one where I reflected on an experience. It was the meaning-of-life kind of introspection where I asked myself questions of truth, but the facts I found did not bring me satisfaction. A feeling of harmony or disharmony was the only barometer by which to judge my life experiences. As I came out of early introspection, I was not the same.

What had been working in my life had stopped working and inertia set in. I needed to move, to feel connected. I was in very good physical shape. My diet was consistent and devoid of unhealthy foods. I gave up drinking wine and coffee. And I was exposing myself to spiritual material in the form of tapes/CDs, books, courses, seminars, and conferences.

I finally decided to do what I had wanted to do coming of out college. I traveled with a backpack but it wasn't really backpacking. I flew business and first class and stayed in nice hotels. I traveled every other weekend for almost two years. Between my trips to various parts of Europe, Asia, South America, North America, and the Caribbean, I attended spiritual conferences and seminars throughout the United States. My consciousness was being shifted. When I envisioned my backpacking trip, it was about meeting people and having a good time. At the speed of life your outcomes are often different from your plans. My sojourns were spent mostly in isolation, meditation, walking, and jogging.

One morning during meditation I was hit with a divine inspiration. I picked up a pen and began to write. The information came fast and it took no more than fifteen minutes. Then I put down my pen and cried.

I wrote *Reminder To Self*.

I was a conduit for this energy. It came through me without my consciousness of its source, or so I thought. What I had written was a reminder to me of what would be important for my life's journey. It was a definition of who I longed to be. I was given a way of being that would bring me peace in the midst of chaos by showing me how to be, regardless of the events of my life. It was a way of being in all my experiences, so that I could be consistent and whole always, in all ways.

I printed two copies and hung one on my closet door and one on my office wall. I shared the insight with a few people and left it at that. The feedback I got was "insightful and inspiring" like an emailed chain letter.

I met my wife, Amanda, at a Debbie Ford three-day intensive seminar. Debbie inspires and teaches people how to love the whole self, the good and the bad, the light and the dark. Amanda and I courted for a short time and married quickly.

It wasn't love at first sight. She was not my usual "type". She was a model and physically attractive—trouble! But inside that book with a beautiful cover there was depth, compassion, and appreciation for life, people, and the little things. I have never met anyone who is as satisfied with little things, like fried plantains, as with the big ones, like diamond earrings. It is amazing who you meet when you put down your judgments and embrace the people who are placed before you.

Amanda found meaning in *Reminder To Self*. She shared it with her father, Dr. C. Bradford Chappell, who was so moved by it that he shared it with a cancer group that he had been facilitating for almost twenty years. They are responsible for this work coming to light. They encouraged me to write *Reminder To Self*.

Writing a book was no small task for me.

I prayed for guidance and got the answer, the same answer Debbie Ford, Deepak Chopra, Wayne Dyer, Brad Chappell, and modern-day spiritual thinkers teach. It is the revelation that Jesus, Krishna, and Buddha gave. It is a truth taught by the mystics—the answers are within.

I had to have a conversation with myself, the same self that was present during the divine inspiration. The same self that has been the quiet observer of all my life. I had to suspend my judgments about this strange idea. Perhaps it was not so strange after all; I seem to have conversations with myself regularly, both in my mind and out loud, and I believe you do too.

Reminder To Self is a conscious conversation with myself during which I elaborate on the inspiration that I received two years earlier. As any normal dialogue unfolds, as many questions were posed as were answered. The dialogue was the agent of great change and understanding for me.

I have come to know that this book is to serve as a tool for others to realize that they too have an inner voice beckoning to be heard, so that life can be fulfilled from the inside out.

This is how the divine insight came out, title and all, on Tuesday, May 24, 2005, at 6:22 in the morning.

Reminder to Self
It is important that you:

Practice self-love
To know love so that you can show love
To have love so that you can give love
To be love so that you can see love

Be deliberate with your choices
So that you can be congruous with your purpose for being

Be in the moment
So that you may experience the perpetual awe of living

Live with integrity
So that you can be consistent and whole in all your experiences

Live in abundance
So that you can give freely and receive freely

Detach from your outcomes
So that you can be courageous with your decisions and let your connection to God manifest its miracles

Open up your heart
So that you can shine your unique light and be a part of the puzzle that you are here to complete

MY STORY: DIVINE INTERVENTION

Live today in joy
Like you have never lived a day and like you will never live another

The process of writing *Reminder to Self* is the process of my transformation. I could not write without experiencing the reminders on many levels. In the two years and five months that it took me to breathe life into this book, I unsettled the sediments of my years of living. I was left with more questions than answers—a wonderful place to be. Then on the final pass, I received the answer, the one that made the most sense of life. It is the essence of every word I have written and it is mentioned in every reminder. I believe it will become clear to you by the time you get to the end of this dialogue and certainly by the end of yours.

Of the infinite paths you could have chosen and the gazillion choices you have made, we meet here. It is my hope that you will be inspired to use these reminders as you continue your journey.

Where am I?
Who am I?
How did I come to be here?
What is this thing called the world?
How did I come into the world?
Why was I not consulted?
And If I am compelled to take part in it,
Where is the director?
I want to see him.

—Soren Kierkegaard

The Wisdom of God Is Within You*

In any given moment we have conversations with ourselves—in the form of silent thoughts, prayer, and meditation—it is perfectly legitimate. However, the moment our internal conversations become audible, we suffer the hypocritical condemnation of the unexamined mind. This results in judgments about the essence of the self. For millennia we have been instructed to look within for the answers to guide us. Instead we have surrendered this endowment to so-called experts and self-proclaimed gatekeepers rather than to a God that exists within us. When we attempt to liberate ourselves, they rebuke us.

* Obviously this dialogue is skewed toward Christianity. There are other spiritual beliefs systems just as valid for those who practice them. However in spite of my awareness and study of them, I still see the world through Christian eyes.

This book is about the liberation of a self that was in captivation by the unknown "they". As we liberate ourselves we liberate others and as we liberate others we liberate ourselves.

Go with me on this; you are not the only one having dialogues with yourself. Human beings are different, but not that different. We gather information through our experiences but our answers will always come from within. We are always connected to Source. Source is God and therein lies your wisdom.

Who am I?

That is a very big question, how do you mean it?

How have I come to conceptualize myself? How do I summarize thirty-nine years in a 30-second elevator speech?

You are an intelligent man who has lived an interesting life filled with adventure, good relationships, surprises, disappointments, failures, successes, love, children, and God. You enjoy learning about and thinking through abstract concepts as they relate to existence and the meaning of life. When your thoughts and actions are purposeful, you find a place of belonging in this world.

What am I?

Again, a very big question but I get it. In physical form you are a human being traveling through this life experiencing the meaning of it.

Beyond that, when I look at myself what do I see? If everything that I know, I was taught, who am I without that training, the knowledge of others? How do I function beyond the sciences? How do I experience myself? What is my consciousness all about? How

> do I relate to others? How do I affect others? That meaning-of-life question—how do I answer it?

Many have pondered these same questions and volumes have been written in attempts to answer them. You can't answer in a sentence or even a paragraph or even volumes of books. To answer that question would make you a master, but the answers are revealed in the student. It's a paradox.

Student. That would be a powerful answer to the question. After all, we are all students of our own lives. It is only through being a student that you can explore and uncover what is already embedded within you. Nothing you will discover is new. It may seem unfamiliar, but it's not new. Understanding is the process of remembrance. To remember requires that you neutralize your misconceptions and trust yourself to have the truth of your experience filter through your truest self and therefore reconnect with the purest part of you—your Source. One word describes who you are—*energy*.

Think about it. Is there a life, a scenery, a movement, an idea, a form, a thing that has no energy? Can anything be created without energy? Can anything be experienced without energy? The only thing that holds us together as a human being is energy. Scientists have discovered that at the most minute levels of our makeup, there is nothing but energy. You are a human being energy. Think about the phrase "mind, body, and soul".

The mind, the body, and the soul refer to the three dimensions of energy. Life is energy. Nothing in this world functions without energy. Even the appearance of no energy is energy at an unobservable point. Nature is held together with an intricate web of energy exchanges, with each form animated by the energy of the next form. The delicate balance of nature is the delicate exchange of energy. Each form is dependent on another. When the balance is thrown off, the world compensates in unimaginable ways, such as wars, global warming, natural disasters, the disappearance of the rain forest, and the extinction of the dinosaurs. Look at the tone of the world; it is one of fear and distrust, fright and fight, and putting the self above all else. We are living in a state of tremendous energy imbalance.

How does my energy affect all of that?

You are a micro-reflection of a macro-condition. As it is within you, it is projected upon the world. Each of us is a powerful source of energy that, when efficiently harnessed, can light up the world like Jesus or leave a dark cloud like Hitler. If Jesus is too big, how about Mother Teresa, Nelson Mandela, Albert Einstein, Mozart, Dr. Martin Luther King, Jr. or Bob Marley? All of them harnessed their energy and moved the world toward peace, a state of energy in balance.

And what about all the people who gave their energy to these icons to help them shine? It is easy to see the icons, the ones that shine, but no one has ever, nor will they ever, achieve greatness without the energy of others. One great person represents only the tip of the human iceberg; beneath is a pyramid of all the shoulders they are standing on to reach their pinnacle. You will always stand on someone else's shoulders and someone else will stand on yours. You are the progeny of those who have gone before you and progenitor of those to come. That is the way of the world.

If you can achieve harmony between the three dimensions of energy (the mind, the body, and the soul), you will radiate a brilliance unique only to you but necessary for the world. When Einstein said, "Nothing happens until something moves," he was talking about energy. We are constantly giving and taking energy from each other.

There are two types of energy, positive and negative or weak and strong. Weak energy or negative energy means you are farther away from Source energy and heading toward darkness. Strong or positive energy means you are closer to source energy and heading toward light. When you reduce your contaminations, such as prejudgments and biases of self and others, you can serve as a conduit for Source or pure energy. You will not be free of contamination in this life. However, greatness is achieved in spite of and sometimes because of your contaminations. None of the icons mentioned earlier, with the exception of Jesus, are without flaws, but they all contributed to making the world a better place to experience life.

Of the three dimensions of energy, the body is the apparatus for physical energy, the mind is the apparatus for mental energy, and the soul is the apparatus for spiritual energy. You need balance within and among the dimensions to experience peace. Your physical apparatus for energy—the body—is your most obvious example of evidence for balance.

The energy you experience on the inside is a reflection of the energy you feed yourself. If you feed your body good energy in the form of healthful food, exercise, and rest, your body will reflect that nurturance with good health and vibrancy. Your world is filled with neglected bodies that are not given the proper nutrition and not exercised and, therefore, suffer from ill health and lethargy.

Your mind requires the same from your external world; whatever you feed your mind in the form of information will be reflected in your thinking and creativity. If your mind is fed light, then it will project light. If it is fed darkness, it will project darkness. You do what you know.

Spiritual energy is unique; it is fueled from the inside. It is the energy that connects you to Source energy. You may share common experiences with others, may practice the same religion, and may believe the same things, but your truth comes from the inside. In each of us resides the knowing of truth. When there is a match from the outside, it serves as a reminder, not knowledge; the knowledge is within. The knowledge comes from Source energy. While your body and mind require external stimulation and sustenance, your spirit is the operating system of your existence.

You are your own spiritual energy, your guide to Source energy. You are unbiased and independent of the circumstances of your life. It is where you turn when you are in need of a connection to something greater than your perceived self. You spend most of your time in the physical and mental dimension. You believe that if your body and mind are strong, then your life will be fulfilled. It doesn't work that way. Without your spiritual involvement in all your doings, it is just a matter of time before a collapse occurs, a mental and physical breakdown of your being that requires a course correction, which requires a spiritual basis to your existence.

Your spiritual energy has always been around as your conscience, companion, confidant, and direct connection to God, where you can find all your answers. Your intuition is your spiritual guide, that little voice in your head. It gives you the answers to everything, but you don't always know how to hear it. When it persists and you do hear it, you don't trust it; you think you are imagining things. Until you can trust yourself about what you know about yourself, you can never trust what you know about others.

> Quite honestly I am just really looking for self-knowledge and understanding; that stuff that makes me tick. Everything I thought I was, I am not. Things that I thought I wanted, I don't. I am thinking that I don't know the person that is emerging. Is it possible to know myself completely?

Your understanding of your life has been distorted. As a student it is the first thing you are to learn. This distortion has come from the unending external influences in your experiences. When you begin to reference your self as a source of truth, you begin to get answers. You will then understand that self-knowledge is knowing who you are based on your current level of exposure to what is possible.

Foundational principles and values, the things that are constant about you, are relative to your experience. When you are aware of yourself, you have a good understanding of your tendencies, feelings, and behaviors. You will spend all your life here on earth working to get to know yourself. You work on self-knowledge because you recognize that there is more to you than you know, so you keep searching. Complete knowledge of self occurs when you know that you don't know everything about yourself. The knowledge is not in the answers, it is in the questions. The more you search, the more you find; and the more you find, the more you search.

If you are fortunate, you will recognize that knowing yourself completely is not truly possible and experiencing yourself fully is more important. Life is about experiencing how you are in the moment. As you become aware of yourself in the moment, you will experience a constant evolution of the self, which is no more different than the evolution of anything else. Change is constant, which means you are constantly changing, so you must be open to how you are, not who you think you are.

"How I am", not "who I am?" What does that mean?

Who you are is different from *how* you are. *Who* you are is fixed in the past. It implies no growth, no evolution, and no observation of your experience in the moment. You are constantly changing, which is the process of evolution. Who you are boxes you into what you have been and what you think you ought to be.

How you are, on the other hand, puts you in observation mode, the student-mind, and allows you to grow based on your experience in the moment. Observing yourself in the moment is the best way of seeing how you experience yourself in the world. Through this self study you come to know yourself by allowing yourself to be.

Knowing yourself is not equivalent to knowing everything that you have done and what you will do. Knowing yourself is being open to knowing that you don't know what you think you know. It is knowing that everything you have been, you are. Everything you thought you were, you are. Everything you thought you were not, you are. The things you thought you wanted, you do. To be a whole person you must embrace all of yourself—the positive and the negative, the desirable and the undesirable. Having a consciousness that you are and that you are not all of those things at the same time is the essence of your wholeness. It is your choice which comes to the fore.

Every good that you see in the world is within you. Every evil that you see in the world is also within you. You get to choose the manifestation of your self. Mother Teresa acknowledged this truth when she said she recognized the Hitler in her, but she made the choice to follow her light. It is the recognition and the embrace of all that you are, good and bad, that leads you to powerful and propelling choices.

The energy that is strongest within you is the energy that you feed yourself and it is the energy you will radiate. An old Cherokee Indian was speaking to his grandson:

> "A fight is going on inside me," he said to the boy. "It is a terrible fight, and it is between

two wolves. One is evil—he is anger, envy, sorrow, regret, greed, arrogance, self-pity, guilt, resentment, inferiority, lies, false pride, superiority, and ego. The other is good. He is joy, peace, love, hope, serenity, humility, kindness, benevolence, empathy, generosity, truth, compassion, and faith. This same fight is going on inside you and inside every other person, too."

The grandson thought about it for a long minute, and then asked his grandfather, "Which wolf will win?"

The old Cherokee simply replied, "The one you feed."

You use your body to experience the physical world, all the material blessings. Your mind is a sponge that absorbs the physical world and draws conclusions from that information. The mind does a magical thing. It not only absorbs information, but it can also interpret the information, check it out against what you remember, and then make contributions back to the world from which it got the original information. Others can then build on this contribution. This is mutual dependency on each other and how progress is made.

The soul is your center. It is your spiritual guide and the purest part of you. It is unchanging, unflinching, and absolutely dependable. When you are conscious of it, it will provide the guidance you need to live a full life. Even so, you will constantly experience the paradoxical life.

> The paradoxical life? Sounds like a great title for a movie but what does this mean?

The duality of your existence brings balance and meaning to your life. The meanings of the concepts in your life are given in relative terms. Good by itself is meaningless, unless and until it is seen in terms of its opposite, bad. These relative terms are usually the ideal states of a concept, compared to their polar opposites; night versus day, fat versus slim, fast versus slow, good versus evil, etc. The paradoxical life is lived when you dance in and out of seemingly contradicting alternatives, equally valuable to your experience. Such is the relationship between your spirit and the ego.

The ego is to the mind as the spirit is to the soul. The ego is the polar opposite of the spirit. Your ego is that part of you that makes you competitive with self and others. It has the tendency to get into places and situations devoid of spirit. As Dr. Chappell explains, "We need ego when we are young to keep us safe. It helps us to know we are not the road, the swimming pool, the cliff, etc. And it lets us know we are not anyone else. At the time of adulthood, we need to start letting go of the ego but it is an intelligent little bugger. When we try to let it go, it gets more important and causes us more pain and the more pain it causes us the more important it becomes. The ego and the 'spirit' have a very difficult time being in the same body simultaneously." If left unchecked and unmanaged the ego can make life difficult and sometimes a living hell.

Let's look at your goal of amassing large quantities of money. You wanted to be a millionaire by the age of thirty—an ego aspiration. That goal became a singular focus in your twenties and it cost you some important relationships. You were not the husband, father, son, or friend you wanted to be and you were not at peace with yourself. You were in debt up to your eyeballs, miserable, and dissatisfied chasing your millions. After looking at yourself and not liking what you saw, you humbled yourself to prayer and meditation which connected you with what was important to you. In pursuing peace, your life changed. The hell your ego created was rescued by the desires of your soul. Your ego aspiration created a void of spirit and an opportunity for you to become conscious about your true desires—and the spirit entered.

When you bring the spirit to places where your ego dwells, you can be propelled to great heights. The goodness you seek for self becomes the goodness you seek for all when the spirit enters the ego domain. It is impossible to eradicate the ego, and you would not want to. The ego as an ally to the spirit creates a great internal partnership that opens a tunnel to our greatness.

When you find that partnership between the two, a self emerges that will help you navigate this world in pure joy. This is where you experience self-love.

> My desire to write *Reminder to Self*, combined with the ego goal of it being a bestseller, is the coexistence of the spirit and the ego. As I write, I speak; the more I speak, the more people I inspire; the more people I inspire, the more books I sell; the more books I sell, the more people I serve. In the process many will benefit and I will connect to my purpose.

Often ego-aspirations are cloaked in the name of goodness. When you seek power in the name of good, you find the ego disguised as the spirit. When the good you do finds a need in places beyond your initial intent and you are compelled to do something about it, your ego and spirit are working together.

> This is the coexistence of the ego and the spirit? My ego seems to get me into places where only my spirit can rescue me. I have had a love and respect for self that I now see has been ego driven. As a result, I have been many things, egotistical, cocky, callous, and selfish.

When you function from a place of self-love, qualities like egotism, cockiness, and callousness disappear. But selfishness is desirable; "selfish" has some redeeming aspects. It has gotten a bad reputation over time; it has come to mean good for the self but inconsiderate of others. Selfless, on the other hand, indicates doing good for others. The problem with selfless is that it takes the self out of doing good; you are selfish, or full of self, for inconsiderateness, but selfless, or absent of self, for doing good. The self is completely present for good and bad—considerate and inconsiderate; what makes the difference is self-love.

Some of the most selfish people to have walked this earth are those who have done the most good: Jesus, Mother Teresa, Gandhi, Nelson Mandela, Dr. Martin Luther King, Jr., and, the most evil, Hitler.

> Jesus is the brightest light that has ever walked on this earth and Hitler is arguably the darkest. Mother Teresa was a saint who brought love and light to all she came across. How can Jesus and Mother Teresa be in the same category with Hitler?

Each of us is placed on this earth as individual parts of a larger puzzle. Our place in this universe, on this earth, in this puzzle called life is unique and necessary. Everything has a purpose. Every purpose is service. Every service is God's work. Even what appears to be disservice is service.

When we are born, we are born with a purpose that must be carried out, regardless of our understanding of it and in spite of our attention to it. The only thing a tree does is be a tree. But, a tree helps balance the ecosystem through photosynthesis by converting carbon dioxide into an energy source and emitting the oxygen our bodies use as energy. Depending on the tree, we may enjoy the fruit it bears as food. Trees have no awareness of their purpose, they just execute at a primal level. That same tree could provide the lumber that builds our homes, our furniture, or toys for our children. The purpose of a tree is to serve.

Humans have the same purpose—to contribute to the existence of the world in a meaningful way. "Meaningful" here is defined as full of meaning, bad or good, at an instinctual base level, such as producing carbon dioxide, and a deliberate preconceived plan, such as finding a cure for cancer.

Like a tree, Jesus couldn't do anything but be Jesus. When we factor in instincts and free will, he came with a specific purpose to be the ultimate example of living with the love of God. Jesus represents everything that is good, therefore he was the most selfish person to ever walk this earth. Jesus could not be anyone but himself. As he fully actualized, the world became the beneficiary of this self. In fulfilling his purpose he was persecuted and eventually killed. He knew he was going to be betrayed and crucified, but he didn't change his actions because he couldn't; he was honoring the self.

This is not a statement about destiny, it is a statement about choice. When you are aligned with your purpose, you are aligned with your truest self. When you are aligned with your truest self, you make choices to support your purpose for being. Jesus was being true to himself and his purpose for being. His purpose was service and his service was the atonement.

Dr. King had the premonition that he was eventually going to be killed for his work toward equal rights for all citizens, but he continued. He too was selfish; he had no other way of being but to fulfill the purpose for which he was born. His purpose was service, his service was civil rights.

Mother Teresa knew of many other ways to live and could have been less selfish and enjoyed a material life, but she chose to live like the people she served, even during the times that she couldn't feel the presence of God. Her purpose was service, her service was dignity of the destitute.

These people were in full alignment—mind, body, and soul—with Source energy. As a result, this trinity of love, including self, other, and God, flowed through them and they shined their unique light in this puzzle called life.

What about Hitler?

Of course, for there to be light, there must be darkness. There is opposition in all things. The truth of Hitler is the truth of Mother Teresa; he was as dark, in relative terms, as she was light. It feels easier for us to see Hitler as selfish but his commitment to his purpose for being was similar to the others. His contribution to mankind is just as profound. Hitler provided the darkness for many to shine their light. The world is more alert and thus safer because of Hitler's evil. A people grew stronger in faith and culture and great fortunes were made that resulted in helping others. The difference between Hitler and the rest of the group was that Hitler was without self-love. Because he did not know the true love for self, he didn't know true love for others and true love of God. Only through ignorance of the trinity of love can such atrocities be perpetrated against mankind, or any kind for that matter.

None of these people performed selfless acts; their entire selves were fully present for the contributions they made. We are led to believe that for good to be done the self has to be absent; not so. We can do good only when the self is present. Only when we filter our experiences through the highest, truest part of each of us will the work we do be of love.

* * *

As I work through the reminders, many things will be made clear. The simplicity of the reminders will surprise you. You will realize that your life lived deliberately will bring joy. Your task will then be to incorporate them more fully into your life by sharing them with others.

Why me?

Why not me and why not you? You are no more or no less special than anyone else. Jesus said, "Even the least among you can do what I have done." That makes you just as capable as you choose to be. You are just as much a conduit of God's energy as I am or anyone else is. Everyone, on some level, is having an internal dialogue. The question is whether it's a constructive or destructive dialogue. Will your dialogue move you closer to or farther from Source?

Let's begin.

To thine own self be true, and it must follow, as the night the day, thou canst not then be false to any man.

William Shakespeare, Hamlet

ONE

Practice Self-Love

*It is important that you practice self love,
to know love so that you can show love,
to have love so that you can give love,
to be love so that you can see love.*

A deep love resides inside each of us. This love is independent of the desires, thoughts, and opinions—good or bad—that are readily offered to us. It is a love that is gentle and kind, accepting and nonjudgmental, playful and spontaneous, courageous and curious. It is always encouraging and always evolving. This love can be discovered only through turning off the noise around us, coming to ourselves in silence, meditation, and prayer. If we listen carefully we will hear the murmurs of our inner voice express yearnings of our truest selves. What we discover is a profound understanding, appreciation, and full acceptance of self—all of the good and all of the bad. Only when we truly know that we are able to tap into this part of ourselves can we begin to love others fully. Love for others is the manifestation of love for self. We cannot love another more than we love ourselves. Life is like a mirror. If we want to know what love for self looks like, we must look at our love for others. If we want to know what our love for others looks like, we must look at our love for self. When we love ourselves this way, we love God this way. And this relationship is the divine love triangle—self, God, and others in any order.

PRACTICE SELF-LOVE

There is a principle for living that is critical to your healthy growth and development but is usually suppressed because cultures and religions scold those who apply it. This same principle is essential to the way that you serve others, be they family, friends, or foes. Implicit in the greatest commandment in the Bible is a truth for which you are chastised. It is the first of eight reminders that must be the cornerstone of your life if you are to be fulfilled. When you *practice self-love* you prepare yourself physically, mentally, and spiritually to live life at your peak and, in doing so, you give the best of you to those who come within your presence.

> I haven't been a fan of the Bible—too much hell, fire, and damnation.

Do these scriptures sound like hell, fire, and damnation to you?

> "Honor thy father and they mother: and Thou love thy neighbor as thy self." Matthew 19:19

> "Thou shalt love the Lord thy God with all thy heart, and with all thy soul, and with all thy strength, and with all thy mind; and thy neighbor as thy self. Luke 10:27

The fact of the matter is your foundation is built upon Biblical principles and specifically Christian principles. But love for others using love for self as the ideal is not just a Christian principle; all religions or spiritual practices espouse this truth as the Golden Rule in one way or another.

> *Judaism:* Thou shalt not avenge, nor bear any grudge against the children of thy people, but thou shalt love thy neighbor as thyself: I am the LORD. Torah Leviticus 19:18
>
> *Christianity:* Do unto others as you would have them do unto you. Matthew 7:12, Luke 6:31, Luke 10:27
>
> *Islam:* None of you truly believes until he loves for his brother what he loves for himself. Muhammad (c. AD 571–632) in a *hadith*
>
> *Hinduism:* This is the sum of duty; do naught unto others what you would not have them do unto you. Mahabharata (5:15:17) (c. 500 BC)
>
> *Buddhism:* Hurt not others in ways that you yourself would find hurtful. Udana-Varga 5,1

Taoism: Regard your neighbor's gain as your gain, and your neighbor's loss as your own loss. Tai Shang Kan Yin P'ien

Confucianism: Do not do to others what you would not like yourself. Then there will be no resentment against you, either in the family or in the state. Analects 12:2

You have been searching all these years for things you had already learned by the time you reached the age of ten. These truths have been imprinted in your heart, which is now beating a tune unfamiliar to you. Remember how important they are, the most important of which is self-love. Before you can love thy neighbors as thyself, you must know what it is to love thyself. The way you love yourself is the way you are to love your neighbor. The things that you do unto others are those things that you would have them do unto you. An understanding of the desires of your soul is necessary before you understand the desires of the souls of others; it requires self-love.

What is it to love thy self? What is self-love?

In order to understand self-love, you need to examine love. Love is energy. Energy always comes from Source. The source of love is God. Only one love comes from

God and it flows through one to another and then back to Source all at the same time. Having self-love is a bit of a misnomer because what you are truly doing is experiencing the love of God, which is constantly flowing, regardless of your awareness of it.

There are no imperfections in this love. The love that binds this universe together is the same love that binds you together—mind, body, and soul. And it is the same love that binds you to one another. It is only your judgments and condemnations that place distance between you and this love. But you are the perfect conduit of this love; it is your birthright.

Look at the fundamental principles of a simple puzzle. Each piece in a puzzle is important for its completion and each position is as critical as the next. Each piece must be in its relative position for the next piece to be in its relative position. Your world works the same way. It is essential that you recognize your importance to other and that each of you is a true conduit of a love that must be fully expressed for the next person to be fully expressed. People without self-love are without love. People without love are without true understanding of God. When you have love, you have self-love and when you have self-love, you have God. Having love is tapping into the ever-flowing love from God and therefore becoming a conduit, a carrier of love. Self-love is God's love directed at you.

PRACTICE SELF-LOVE

> What is the practice of self-love? How do I experience this love? Is it a thought, a feeling, or an action? I have intellectually wrestled with the term "being in love." It seems impossible to get there and stay there.

Love is all of those things; a thought and a feeling that is experienced through an action—essentially, energy. When it is self-directed, you have self-love. Being "in love," as you know it, is actually being in a temporary state of love like other temporary states, such as sadness, anxiety, or bewilderment. Being in a temporary state of love, which you call "being in love," occurs when your circumstances are ideal to the self mentally and physically at the same time. In many cases you even have a spiritual experience while being in this temporary state of love.

When you are with the one your heart desires, sharing experiences that are expressions of the feeling of happiness, you are in a temporary state of love. Being in a temporary state of love this way is not unique to a romantic relationship. You feel this love in all relationships—platonic, intimate, familial, or anything to which you relate. Talking on the telephone with a friend and truly connecting produces a temporary state of love. Embracing your wife in a gentle hug as your connection moves beyond the surface level is being in a temporary state of love. Holding hands during a leisurely stroll with your daughter produces feelings of being in a temporary state of love. When you are in awe at a natural landscape, you are in a temporary state of love. Being in a temporary state of love requires conditions conducive to experiencing good feelings at a conscious level. These good feelings ignite the senses and produce the feeling of love.

True love, on the other hand, is really being in God's love. It is tapping into the love that is available to you directly from Source and indirectly through others. It is being in constant awareness and appreciation of the magnificence of your world and yourself as a critical part of that world. When you are in love this way, the conditions of your life do not have to be ideal for the experience of love. The level of love is at the conscious and subconscious level as a way of being. The conditions around you do not produce a feeling of love; you bring love to the conditions around you. Physical, mental, and spiritual comfort are not required for you to experience love because the love comes through you as a conduit of a greater love, the Source of love, God. This love is the love that connects all humanity together.

The self is the effect of the body, mind, and spirit. Self-love is the full, unconditional love and acceptance of all that you are. Recognition that you are not just a conduit of Source love but also a receiver of it is self-love; the love you are to give to others has also been given to you. As a conduit of love you are free of interference because there is no time or space between you as a conduit and a receiver of it.

Interference comes in the form of mental, physical, and spiritual imperfections. When you remember self-love, you have no interference. You see yourself as being whole, regardless of perceived imperfections. When you unconditionally love yourself, you are kind, gentle, caring, compassionate, honest, and real with yourself. You are without judgment and condemnation of yourself. When you are this way with yourself, you are this way with others. You can pursue your dreams and achieve them without compromising others. Your successes can never be lasting if you compromise others to get it. Your successes serve as the gateway for others to succeed. If you do not succeed, you will prevent others from succeeding through you.

When you have self-love, your actions are reflective of those things that will connect you to Source; actions that connect you to Source connect you to others.

What about when my acts of love threaten others and are viewed as selfish?

At times, your expression of self doesn't fit the image others have of you and threatens the image or box in which you have been placed. As long as you are earnest in your doings and are guided by truth, love, and sincerity, you do not need to be afraid of the opinions of others.

When you love yourself, some people may consider it selfish, but when you love yourself you honor yourself. When you honor yourself, you honor others because you give your whole self. You express your truest desires. You establish your boundaries. People know where you stand. Honoring yourself is the only way to truly honor others. Love for others must be filtered through love for self.

Accordingly, you teach people how to treat you. By honoring yourself you demonstrate to others how to honor you. It is impossible to give what you don't have; you must have love to give love. Everyone comes into this world with an abundant supply of love and yet everyone has a need for this love—another paradox. A baby needs love unconditionally to grow and gives love unconditionally as it grows.

You can tap into the well of love that is inside you when you understand that you are a sanctuary for practicing love. You can also align with the energy of love that surrounds you. What you cannot do is have someone else define love for you. If you do, you are at the mercy of someone else's definition, which is a false image of you. If you tap into the love that is available to you, you will know love first-hand.

How do I tap into the love that is available to me?

You are doing it now. You are having a deep dialogue with yourself. Prayer and meditation will also connect you to your truest self. You need only find a quiet place to be and give your truest self the opportunity to meet you in uncommon ways—ways that you will eventually recognize when you suspend your judgments about what is possible and become open to the impossible.

The spirit in you is the God in you. Regardless of the way you choose to connect to Source, you must shut out the distractions around you and delve within yourself. Quiet contemplation will lead you to a truer self filled with the spirit of God. Inside, you will find your purest desires and a way to fulfill your purpose for being here.

There are people on this earth who are beacons for others. Study their teachings and bathe in the love they have provided and the light they let shine—the great spiritual teachers past and present, including Jesus, Buddha, Krishna, Muhammad, the Dalai Lama, the Pope, Joseph Smith, and your modern-day prophets and mystics. Surround yourself with inspirational people and inspirational material. If you want to see what you look like, look at the people with whom you surround yourself. If they are not the type of people you would like to be, move on. Your experiences will validate your beliefs, so be deliberate about the choices you make.

> And what of unconditional love? I don't believe it exists. It seems like people give more or less love based on what you do for them. If you please them,

> you get praised and loved, but if you displease them, that love is lessened or withdrawn altogether.

Love is. It cannot be decreased or increased. When you are in true love, you love regardless of the conditions. This is unconditional love; being in God's love. When you are in a temporary state of love, you love because of the conditions. When the conditions change, love is withdrawn.

In loving you, do others love the truest part of you or do they love an idea of you that represents themselves—how are they pleased by you? Many parents, out of love, want their children to be brilliant lawyers, doctors, and other professionals. These parents send their children to the best schools for training even if the child wants to be a farmer or an artist. You have experienced well-intentioned people loving you in ways they believe to be best, but the love doesn't honor the truest part of you. This kind of love is conditional and confusing. Many people give love based on the desires of their hearts, not yours, and it's misguided. How they love comes from good intentions and what they believe you need to be loved. In reality, many people give to get rather than serve the relationship.

If your love for self is conditional, you will create experiences where love of others will be conditional, and their love of you will also be conditional. When you were the leader of your company and a leader in your community, you made friends with people in high places. You lived a life based on the title and position you held and associated with people of similar ilk. After you left your company, you disassociated yourself from those interactions because you no longer had the same aspirations and little to offer. In fact, you had much to offer. You confused your positional power with your personal power, confusing what you did for a living with how you are.

You will find the same confusion in athletes when the stadium lights are turned off or in celebrities when the curtain closes and their careers come to an end. Not only are they regarded with less fanfare by others, they begin to think of themselves as being worth less than when they were stars.

When love for self is conditional, others will love you conditionally. It is energy and it radiates from you. When you struggle to love and fully accept the self, you struggle to love and fully accept others. Life is like a mirror. What you do to self is what you do to others. When you love yourself, you show people how to love you and with that they know how to support you.

The mother who holds her young child all day without regard for herself as a human being who needs quiet time, exercise, and to be loved herself is a martyr. She cannot fully love that child if she neglects herself to do it. The self must be healthy for the cycle of love to flow. In order to be whole you must be mindfully engaged in fully supporting and satisfying your truest self, that God-like self who came to this earth to manifest a unique experience and to share your unique gift with the world.

You have a contribution to make. It doesn't matter what your situation is in this life; it doesn't matter what your background is, what your material standing or previous experiences are; and it doesn't matter if you were loved all your life or abused for part of it. Right now, your true self awaits reconciliation in order to magnify your purpose and be at one.

You must start with self-love, which is God's love, unconditionally accepting, loving, and living with the deepest part of you, your soul. It is only when you love yourself this way that you can love others this way. When you have love for yourself and others, you will have love for God and complete the divine love triangle. Practicing self-love requires that you *be deliberate with your choices,* a process that aligns you with a specific way to execute your purpose here on earth.

I went to the woods because I wished to live deliberately, to front only the essential facts of life, and see if I could not learn what it had to teach, and not, when I came to die, discover that I had not lived.

Henry David Thoreau, Walden

TWO

Be Deliberate With Your Choices

*So that you can be in alignment
with your purpose for being.*

We have been blessed with the gift of choice and with this gift we determine our life's journey. The gift of choice is the key to personal empowerment. Choosing is not an option, for we either choose a thing or we don't choose a thing, whichever we do is our choice. Therefore, we create the choices we make or select from those that are left to us. Because we have to choose anyway, it is in our best interest, and that of our universe, that we make our choices deliberately.

The trees, oceans, rivers, and sun are unique and purposeful pieces of the intricate puzzle called life and, like those natural elements, we too are unique pieces with a gift; a talent; a way to fulfill purpose. Understanding how to love ourselves through the choices we make will unlock the doors to our magnificence, not by the definition of man, but by the definition of the universe and its need for us. Our gift of choice is the first recognition of self-determination and the single most powerful tool that we are given to navigate this world.

The second principle you must remember is that you have the ability to choose. If you make all your choices deliberate, you will engage your purpose for being in this life.

> I know I always have a choice. It is one of those foundational principles for self-development.

Do you truly know that? The only true result of knowledge is change. When you know a thing, you come to understand the explicit and implicit meaning of it, and when you come to truly know a thing this way, you are changed by it. You change in your thoughts, beliefs, attitudes, and actions. You understand intellectually that you have choices, but you don't understand that in every moment of your life you are making choices.

In every moment you act or you are acted upon which makes you the creator of your destiny or the victim of it. The profundity of this understanding must seep into your consciousness and not be stored as information. Knowledge without change is only information. True knowledge requires change and change requires action. In the past, the action you chose to take led down the path of least resistance, which required no change and you lived an unfulfilled life.

What exactly is meant by the path of least resistance?

There is a great book by Robert Fritz, *The Path Of Least Resistance,* that thoroughly explains this idea. The path of least resistance is taken when you do not deliberately navigate your life but instead follow a path that has been established or presents the least challenge. Here are a couple of examples. A man becomes a doctor because his parents will pay only for medical school, not for an education in the arts, which is what he truly desires. Instead of getting a job and working through college to fund his education in the arts, he becomes a doctor. Similarly, a girl has abusive parents and life is tough. She takes to a life of underachievement and mediocrity because people don't expect much from her and she doesn't give much. She didn't know that at any moment she could make choices to live a different life with a different outcome based on the determination of a self with a definite purpose.

There are at least three ways information will materialize during your experience of life. You can react to your experiences in life; you hear a loud noise, you run. You can respond to an experience; you hear a loud noise, you look, you decide what to do. Or you can create your experiences; you hear a loud noise because it's you playing the drums.

In other words, you can wait for things to happen, you can watch things happen, or you can make things happen. The latter person lives life deliberately. The path of least resistance is taking actions that require the least amount of effort, even if they lead nowhere and especially if they lead somewhere you don't want to go.

When you are deliberate with your choices, your decisions are not expedient but a part of a system, a way of being that is guided by your truest self. The actions you take serve all the relationships in your life—you, God, and others.

> I once met a man in Jamaica on vacation. I struck up a conversation with him and discovered he was a brain surgeon. After talking for a while, I discovered all he wanted to do was to become a farmer. He had bought some land in the South and wanted to farm it, but obligations to his sacrifices, training, and social status prevented him from leaving a highly regarded profession to take up farming.

When your reference for self is external, then your path of least resistance is external. That is, you move with the crowd simply because it is moving, without thought to where it's going, why, and if that is where you want to go. When your reference is internal, your path of least resistance is also internal; you make choices based on your truest self, and even difficult choices are made with the integrity of an aligned soul. In living fully, your path of least resistance is based internally on a way of being that brings light to you, to others, and, therefore, to God.

> The integrity of an aligned soul. What precisely is that, and what is the relationship between integrity and choice?

Integrity is the bedrock of your whole person. When you have integrity, your choices are based on your guiding principles, which have internal reference points. That means you are consistent in thoughts, deeds, and actions, regardless of your circumstances.

Your choices lead to actions that produce experiences, which form or reform your beliefs. Your beliefs form or reform your attitudes, and your attitudes form or reform your choices, which lead to your actions, and the cycle repeats itself.

> So which comes first, the chicken or the egg? Choices, actions, experiences, beliefs, and attitudes. They all seem to influence each other.

It doesn't matter which comes first. You have free will regardless of where you are in the cycle and free will is your ability to choose. The real question is when did you become aware of your free will? The awareness of your ability to choose, regardless of your circumstances, will be your critical moment. For example, let's review some of the choices you made and see how they evolved.

You were brought up poor. You discovered the stigma attached to poverty when your family migrated to the United States. You reacted to your circumstances by choosing to become rich. That was your critical moment; you realized that you had choices, free will. Because you wanted to be rich you were open to ways of getting there. You went to college because you were told the best way to become rich is through an education. While in college you were exposed to all types of information that supported your choice. You believed you were on the road to wealth.

You also believed college students became more successful than non-college students and you developed an attitude reflecting that belief. Sometimes, and usually, that attitude took on an air of superiority; it could have been confidence, but it was definitely different from what it was before college. From your attitudes came your actions; you then applied for the job that would help you amass the fortune you set out to get in the first place.

After a few years, you realized that working for a company was not the best way to gain wealth. You learned that the probability of creating wealth was greater if you relied on your own resources than if you continued working for a corporation, so you started your own company. You needed employees, more knowledge, and capital, so you made a whole set of other choices within your new circumstances. And thus, the cycle repeats itself.

> This is where I get confused. I am in a great place in my life and would not change my experiences, because that's how I got here. Were my choices not deliberate?

Yes, of course; there is no judgment, just a look at your journey. If you had to make those choices again, you would make the same choices because of your system of reference at that time, but you would not make those choices now. You understand much more now than you understood then.

You were deliberate with your choices, but your reference was external. Your choices were based on the fear of poverty, not based on you truest self, by which you are now mindfully guided. Overcoming poverty is no longer your main motivator. Connecting with your purpose is your principle motivation. It is around that ideal you are now making choices. The choices you made a few years ago were driven by how much money you could make. You are not ignorant of your need for money, but you are mindful of your calling to the service of your fellow man as a unique and necessary part of the puzzle. It is much bigger than your egotistical aspirations.

Being deliberate with your choices aligns you with your purpose for being. Your journey contains indirect paths and dead-end trails that serve as your guideposts for getting back to your purpose. Sometimes you have to lose your way in order to find yourself.

What is the relationship between choice and purpose?

Your purpose precedes your choices. When you are disconnected from your purpose, your choices are chaotic and expedient. Every choice you make is made to satisfy a fundamental need. Your fundamental needs are your driving needs. Unless you develop a relationship with your truest self, these fundamental needs drive you without your awareness of them. Beneath your every action is a desired outcome, which may be conscious or unconscious to you. Have you ever done something and afterwards wondered why? Behind that action was a fundamental need at work.

As a human being you want to be fulfilled in your life; you need to belong and be safe, secure, and express yourself. You need to be safe in your physical surroundings. You need good health, food, shelter, and clothing—the basics. You also need to be secure, which means having no threats to your freedom, health, employment, and property. You have a need to belong to a group, whether it is a family, a community, a church, or a fan club of a sports team. You need to love and be loved.

Finally you need to express yourself where you can uniquely contribute to the welfare of others—this is your purpose.

When you practice self-love, which is recognizing that you have the love of God in you and that you are a conduit of this love, you will function from a place that enables you to fulfill your fundamental needs. The choices you make will be aligned with that divine love triangle—you, God, and others. You will have basic needs met, safety needs met, and security needs met, and you will be purposeful in your expression of self through work or otherwise. You will not live a life that is untrue to you.

If you make choices that lead to experiences that move you away from Source, you will make other choices until you are moving toward Source. If you are in circumstances that are unfavorable to you, you will recognize that you can make choices to find more favorable circumstances. The decision to stop chasing your millions is a good example of this truth. Playing the game of making money without providing commensurate service placed you in a situation where you had to choose between what felt right and what felt wrong. Bailing people out of foreclosure on their homes just to line your pockets with their equity, although legal, felt wrong and would take you away from Source. Educating people on responsible homeownership felt good. It hasn't lined your pockets with nearly the same amount of money as the foreclosure business would have, but it took you back to Source and you maintained your integrity.

What happens when these fundamental needs are not met?

When your fundamental needs are not met, they will continue to drive your choices, but often in a direction away from your purpose. You will exist in a state of ignorance where you react or respond to the events of your life rather than creating the desires of your truest self. You will continue to be an unconscious accomplice of your circumstances, rather than the conscious creator of your life experiences. You will have meaningless jobs, participate in things you don't believe in, stay silent when you or others are dishonored, and stay in abusive or empty relationships.

There are people involved in relationships that are not satisfying to their soul—sometimes not to their mind or body either—but they continue to be involved despite knowing the relationship has veiled the true self. They tolerate mediocrity and sometimes abuses when they are not functioning from the truest self. That's what happens when there are fundamental needs working; there are unconscious needs being met in unhealthy ways. This fact becomes evident when we look at the many people addicted to sex, drugs, and alcohol.

Are we all shaped by the circumstances of our lives?

How your circumstances shape your life is totally up to you. There are people born into great wealth who achieve even greater wealth. Others born into similar circumstances choose to follow a path independent of their wealth, simpler and less reliant on the things money can afford. Still, like you, there are people born into poverty who have gone on to live accomplished lives, even create great wealth. The lives of Oprah Winfrey and J. K. Rowling exemplify this point. Oprah rose from poverty and all types of abuse to create great change in the lives of many, amassing a fortune while doing it. She has become the richest woman in the world according to some accounts. Harry Potter was created in the mind of J. K. Rowling who is reported to have been a single mother on welfare when she wrote the bestselling novel that launched the series. She is now a billionaire, the first person to gain such wealth from writing.

It's obvious that wealth is a measure of success in life.

It is, but it is not the only measure. In fact it is the least significant measure, much to the surprise of many. Wealth is a tool and if it is used properly, it can enrich the lives of many; for that matter, so is poverty.

Poverty can enrich lives?

Certainly. Poverty and wealth are different sides of the same coin, a duality of your existence. The world has come a long way because of poverty. Many of the greatest inventors, doctors, writers, musicians, and other agents of change were motivated by poverty. Your circumstances can be a blessing or a curse, and it's your exercise of choice that determines which. Take a look at the life of Oprah Winfrey. Among her many philanthropic efforts is a school in South Africa for underprivileged girls. The lives of those girls will never be the same, the lives those girls touch will be many. Oprah's poverty has driven her and her legacy is remarkable. Bob Marley rose from the poverty of Trench Town, Jamaica, to create a music that touches the lives of many and crosses racial, social, and economic lines worldwide.

And what about Jesus? He was born into poverty and look what he did.

Choices may lead to goals and goals are desired outcomes. Because of your life circumstances, you chose to go to college. That choice became the goal of graduating which then became your desired outcome. You decided upon a series of steps that you needed to complete which were your actions to achieve your goal. You worked on them with a singular focus until you got your college diploma.

Goals are not always achieved, but sometimes are replaced by other goals uncovered during the process of working toward your desired outcomes. As a result of your experiences, you discovered that you are better at inspiring people than managing them. That served as an impetus for becoming an inspirational speaker and that brings you more joy than managing ever did. Do your very best and let the process of achieving your goals unfold. You will gain insight into yourself that can only be discovered in that process. Along the way, check in with yourself to see if what you are doing is satisfying to your soul. Stay detached from your desired outcomes and find your remarkable self.

Goals lead to action and actions have consequences. Like the ripples from one pebble thrown in a pond, a small action can have great consequences. You are free to choose your actions, but you cannot choose the consequences. When you started your spiritual journey back to self, you had no idea of the possibilities to which you would be exposed. You now have a wife and three little girls as a direct result of specifically focusing on your spirit. That's a big ripple!

> So actions have consequences, and I can choose what actions to take, but I can't choose the consequences. Does that mean achieving my goals is a crapshoot?

No, achieving your goals is not a crapshoot. The achievement of your goals is in direct proportion to your understanding and commitment to them. Your idea of the goal and the achievement of it are two different experiences. The achievement of your goals is about making choices and, irrefutably, a choice requires action. It is the idea that nothing happens until something moves and things are always happening because there is always movement. The only uncertainty is whether you will be deliberate with your choices so that the actions you take are consistent with the goals you set and the truest part of yourself.

Even choices that are of the truest self can have unintended, undesirable, and, sometimes, dire consequences. Look at the lives of Jesus, Gandhi, and Dr. Martin Luther King, Jr. Their choices cost them their lives. The converse is also true; seemingly ill-advised choices have desirable consequences. There is an important point to remember; life happens in moments and moments are snapshots, not the entire picture. Your choices and their consequences are a part of your journey, regardless of what they are.

All lives are magnificent stories, especially the seemingly unimportant ones; all have dramas enough to write many bestsellers. People are authors of their own bestselling lives and get to influence the many story lines with the choices they make and the actions they take.

> Choices are hard to make sometimes. When I start thinking beyond money and work, choices become complicated.

Choices are not hard to make when you stand for something, when you know what you are doing here on earth. When you filter the information that comes at you through the truest part of you, then knowing what to choose is simple. Sometimes the perceived outcomes will be unpleasant and undesirable, but the choices are not hard to make.

> Okay, why shouldn't I be confused about that statement?

Sometimes you are faced with a set of choices to which the outcomes will not be pleasant. When you filter the information through the truest part of you, the choice becomes simple, based on your values, but the outcome is still unpleasant. For example, when you dissolved your business partnership, you decided not to allow it to get dirty, even if it cost you everything. There were times when you realized that you would lose more than you thought, but to fight would bring about negative energy that would have pulled you and your family away from Source at a time when you were closest to it. You chose not to fight and, as a result, lost a fortune, but you were true to yourself. The outcome was financially devastating, but the choice, with all things considered, was an easy one to make, once you decided what was important to you and your family.

The important questions to answer are the following: Do your choices lead you to God or away from God? Will your choices serve you, God, and humanity? Your full understanding of your relationship with self, God, and others is critical to making your choices deliberate. The meaning of choices becomes apparent as you filter through the truest part of you. As you have meaning in your choices, you develop meaning in your life. Choices from the truest part of you will lead to God.

> As I find meaning in my choices, will I find meaning in my life?

Sure, the people who struggle with meaning-of-life questions are the people who struggle with meaningful choices. When you chose your life's journey based on your poverty, you made the choice to go to college and from there you ended up an entrepreneur in a "meaning-of-life" crisis. Your choices were based on a reaction to your circumstances instead of coming from your truest self. If you are deliberate with your choices, which are based on awareness of self and its foundational values of love and charity, then you have no issues with the meaning of life. You get to choose what life you live.

You get to choose the meaning of your life. You get to make meaningful life choices.

> What hasn't been said in this dialogue is that it will require an incredible amount of self-control to be deliberate with my choices. I am not aware of the self in a way for this knowledge to be easy to incorporate into my life.

Self-control is a misnomer. You don't need to control the self. On the contrary, you must express the self; that is what you were born to do. Instead, you must have emotional control. Many people are slaves to their emotions and because there are so many emotions, they go mad.

The good news is that when you function from your truest self you have an enormous amount of self-love. When you remember and live the principles we are discussing, you will create a way of being that results in the appropriate emotional expressions, the emotions that reflect your true state of being. You will realize that it's not the events of your life that cause pain and suffering, it is your interpretation of the events of your life that causes you pain and suffering. With this realization you will see things as they are, instead of from a skewed perspective, which is typically what causes a loss of emotional control.

When you are in an experience, good or bad, you use your mind to interpret the experience. Your emotional state will result from what you tell yourself about the experience, not necessarily the actual experience itself.

Your choices can be made only in the present moment. As you are deliberate with your choices, your life will become an exciting puzzle of which you are part. Every choice you make leads you to other choices you must make. The beauty of your life is that your choices have consequences and you can keep choosing until you experience the outcomes that bring you joy. If your choices don't kill you, they will make you stronger.

Regardless of your predicament, you can choose to live your life in a way that is more pleasing to you. Self-love has to be at the core of it and everyone, regardless of background and circumstances, gets to make choices to live a life full of joy.

When you are deliberate with your choices you align yourself with your purpose of being and then your life will happen in moments. When you recognize you have this gift you will spend your time *being in the moment*.

Trust no future, howe'er pleasant!
Let the dead past bury its dead!
Act,—act in the living Present!
Heart within and God o'erhead.

Henry Wadsworth Longfellow,
Psalm of Life

THREE

Be In The Moment

*So that you may experience the
perpetual awe of living.*

Life happens in moments. In every moment our purpose awaits its destiny. This moment, this time, this now is the only place from which we can choose and, therefore, the only moment from which to create.

We explore a thought, generate an action, live, and manifest a destiny in the now. Lessons from the past and plans for the future are our present—in-the-moment experiences. Reflection on our experiences and ultimate growth occur in the now.

When we are deliberate with our choices, our desire is to live in the moment, where we experience the blooming of our creations and the joy of being right where we are. If where we are is where we want to be, then we experience the perpetual awe of living.

The next reminder is the stage from which your greatness is created. It is the great equalizer and the foundation of hope. The greatest accomplishments from the greatest achievers happen one moment at a time and each moment is the present moment in time, the only moment that you can manipulate to live life fully.

> How do I live in the moment when I'm thinking about goals and living deliberately?

We talked about self-love and that without it you can't trust yourself. Self-love focuses you on understanding the self; you are patient, kind, accepting, honoring, and hopeful. Life's duality and your humanity determine that you are the opposite of those qualities as well—impatient, mean, judgmental, fearful, and so on. You get to choose your way of being and what you do to yourself, you do to others. When you feel secure and loving toward yourself, those around you benefit from your kindness. However, there is very little love and kindness for others when you feel insecure, judgmental, and condemning of yourself. Your daughters know this all too well.

When you feel good about yourself, they are the apple of your eye. When you are unsettled and self-doubting, their behavior seems to irritate you. They can't seem to get it right at the dinner table; they slouch, they eat with their mouths open, they shovel their food into their mouths, and their six- and seven-year-old chatter sounds to you like fingernails on a blackboard.

When you truly have self-love, you recognize that you are whole as you are. With this realization, being in the moment is essential in living a full life. And it's not just being in the moment, but also being present and focused. You recognize how blessed you are to come home to your three little girls who are, as you were at their age, beacons of light in a blessed life.

> Yes, it seems like I waste time feeling sorry for myself while projecting my feeling of inadequacy onto the people around me, especially my girls.

Many people live a life of hovering; waiting for the illusion of perfection in order to experience happiness. You may be waiting for a promotion, to lose weight, to gain weight, to get out of debt, to buy a house, to have kids, for the kids go to college; the list is endless. Waiting for goals to be realized is a part of living, but you peg your happiness on the realization of goals. Because the attainment of goals is off in the distance, you spend your moments passing time or obsessing about the happiness you think you'll achieve once those goals are realized, instead of living life fully.

You convince yourself, use your mind to trick yourself into thinking that you are not good enough until the conditions of your life match the picture of it.

> I spent quite a bit of time convincing myself that I could not be a writer until I got a Ph.D. I wanted to study my beliefs in order to validate my thinking; go figure that one. I didn't think I had the qualifications to write about the fundamentals of living a full life. I defeated myself before I started. I felt I had nothing valuable to say, without the proper credentials.

You think you are not good enough until certain conditions are met, so no one is good enough without the right conditions. You do what you know. The same standards to which you hold yourself are the same standards to which you hold others. Programming from society is that status defines you. This is wrong! You do not need a Ph.D. to master your own thoughts.

The standards to which you hold yourself are necessary for your personal and professional development. Mastery of a specific body of knowledge or skill is necessary to magnify your talent. Such mastery becomes a part of you, but it doesn't define you. You must realize that you are whole, valid, capable, and good enough right now, in this moment, with or without credentials. It takes this moment to create a life, not the past and not the future.

> It seems like the past is the greatest predictor of my future, with training and pedigree playing essential roles. But in reality I live between the past

and the future. I have the evidence of the past and the promise of the future, but I seem to live in the uncertainty of the present.

The past would seem like the greatest predictor of the future, just as it seems like the present is uncertain. In truth, the past is often a poor predictor of the future and the present is your most certain indicator. The present, in this moment, is where you manifest your destiny.

With all the technological triumphs, man still has not figured out how to travel back to the past or into the future. Your gift of choice is the greatest tool for navigating this complex world and choosing to live in the moment is critical to your being.

When you get stuck in the past, you replay the choices that didn't materialize as you envisioned, not realizing that those choices worked out exactly as they should have. The greatest stories are told and legends are made in the past, but history occurred in yesterday's present moments, where great failures and triumphs were the result of acting in those moments. You recount the past selectively, omitting or including subtle yet crucial details that embellish your experiences for the better or dramatizing them for the worse. What you are left with are justifications for escaping your present circumstances, making you a victim and rendering you powerless, oblivious to realizing that you are most powerful by living in the now.

BE IN THE MOMENT

> What about being affected profoundly by experiences, such as a great failure, being victimized, or being abandoned by a parent? These experiences have a paralyzing effect on confidence, ability, and courage.

These experiences are all unique to the individual and cannot be felt or experienced in the same way by anyone else. As you have been taught, experience is the perfect teacher, but you are not always a good student. There is a constant dialogue between you and your life, where you tell life how things should be and life tells you how things are. The result of your dialogue with life is either harmony or disharmony. Disharmony is painful but wrought with many lessons. Your responsibility is to keep going, find new ways of expressing yourself until you find the expression that flows with life and satisfies your soul.

The past is a reference, stored information. You must look back only to extract the wisdom from those experiences that help you make deliberate choices in the present moment. When you were two years old you tried to grab fire and you got burned! Today you don't grab fire. It's simple. You can never nor should you ever try to discard your past. Remember, you are an accumulation of all your experiences. You need those experiences to be you; otherwise who would you be?

Your greatest life is not in the past, nor is it in the future. Your greatest life is in the present moment.

Now, is where you determine how to find harmony with life and where you are able to move deliberately toward your desired state of being. Your best life is happening now. Even your memories and dreams are experienced through the mind in the present.

> If I can't live for the future, how do I create a new life or a desirable outcome, especially when my circumstances are dire?

The future is a place for goals and aspirations and where plans are stored, but to get there you need to live and create in the present. There is no way to get to the future without living in the now. The greatest of plans are useless without execution in the present. Many people talk about what they will do and be someday, but they must do and be what they plan for in the present. If you wanted to be a great writer someday, the only way to get there is by writing today. If you picture yourself in the future as being fit and healthy, then you must make fit and healthy choices today, in all your present moments.

You may need help and guidance, but you must begin right now to do whatever you desire for the future. Remember, the future can never be experienced in the future. Life is a series of moments and whatever you want for the future, you must execute in the present. Every deliberate moment creates opportunities for the next moment. Even when you get to the future, you will still be living in the moment, a moment manifested through deliberate execution of present-time activities. You must begin where you are; it is impossible to begin anywhere else.

> The idea that I can only live in the present sounds simple, but it's confusing when I'm living the effects of my past, hoping to better it in the future.

That is precisely the confusion experienced by many people because the mind tricks the self. The present moment is the only place where you can make things happen. You experience the past and future in your mind. A past, experienced in the mind, will keep you stuck, unless used as a reference to help you now. A future, experienced in the mind, is a blueprint for a desired state of being and can derail you, if not executed in the present. If you are stuck because of past experiences, then you have not identified and gathered the gifts from those experiences. Every experience brings the gift of guidance to you, to help you find your way. For instance, your departure from your business gave you the gift of time and focus to follow your dream of writing and teaching.

> If the present is the only place to make things happen, this is the only place from which I can choose.

All choices are made in the present. If you want to see how you got to where you are, look back. If you want to see where you are going, look at what you are doing now.

> The choices I make today, right now, in this moment, determine what kind of future I will live.

Precisely. You get to create the truest self; only you can do that for you. You can define and redefine how you are right now. Because life happens in this moment, you get to be how you are and decide how you are not.

> Is this the logic that says I can be anything I want to be?

Yes, but it's not true. Being is different from doing. In being, your body, mind, and soul are in alignment with what you are. It is a part of your essence. When you are doing, you may have the necessary qualifications through training and experience, but your body, mind, and soul may be out of alignment with that way of being. This is the brain surgeon who wants to be a farmer; this is the businessman who wants to be a teacher; this is the school principal who wants to be a homemaker; and this is the politician who wants to make a difference.

To answer the question, you can accomplish most goals if you are willing to pay the price in the form of choices. Are you willing to pay the price for what the self desires? The idea of a thing and the experience of that thing are different. Before you got married, you and your wife had the best intentions for your marriage. You talked about your dreams, children, vacations, family, etc. You got married and the reality of your marriage conflicted with the dream you had envisioned. Your dreams need money to finance them, your children annoy you sometimes, your vacations seem to exist as dreams, and your family doesn't quite follow the plans you laid out for them—not how you envisioned it. Still you have love, commitment, a great family, and a life of faith—a great foundation from which to build anything.

Can you reconcile the idea of it with the reality of it?

If you are functioning from your truest self, you can create how you are and be that, starting today. The moment you decide to achieve something, you are just moments away from that achievement; all you have to do is chip away at those moments. It sounds simple, but creating your desire is that simple. Live every moment deliberately toward what you desire and you will achieve it. Your moments may be challenging at times, but simply keep moving deliberately toward what you want in order to achieve it. The Bible says, "As a man thinketh so is he." What follows is "As a man does," so is he. Your actions will follow your thoughts. If you don't like what you are doing, then find something that connects to the truest part of you and do that.

> This is more than I was looking for and elevates the question to another level. I simply wanted to know if it is true that I can accomplish anything I set out to do?

No.

> This contradicts conventional inspirational and motivational wisdom. Many people depend on this idea, including me.

You have been misguided. Just because you want to be a tree doesn't mean you will become one. You can't be a car or a rock, and *you* can't be the President of the United States because you weren't born here. You can't be Michael Jordan, as much as you love basketball, and you can't be Bill Cosby—you're just not that funny.

You can only be what you can be. It's never someone else. It's never something else. Just you, and then more of you. But your possibilities are immeasurable.

You can accomplish great things if you are willing to be focused until those goals are reached. That may mean experiencing countless numbers of failures, making tremendous sacrifices, and even creating unimaginable change in the self and society. If you place your mind on a single focus and make choices in your moments, you can achieve great things. If, however, your goals are externally focused, you will not have enduring satisfaction, if any. Many people have multiple careers and life changes for this reason. The idea of a thing and the thing itself are two different experiences. Your Masters degree in psychology is a good example of this point. You enjoyed your classes and expanded your mind immensely, but the idea of counseling for you was different than the act of it.

> So achieving the wrong goal or missing it altogether is not failure?

"No one fails at anything until he or she chooses to act in ways that create failure. People often don't accomplish their goals for many reasons, but the most common is impulse" said Brad Chappelle. Essentially, the goals aren't conceived from the truest self. Goals not of the truest self serve as guiding experiences. Their perceived success or failure is there to give more information about the self. Eventually, with enough information from accomplishing or missing these goals, you understand your dispositions and tendencies, which will guide you to fulfilling your purpose.

Your self-worth has been identified closely with your accomplishments. It's the reason you got your Masters degree; it's the reason your created your own company; and it's the reason you wanted a Ph.D. If you are honest with yourself, you will realize that all of your goals were based on how others would see you and how you would feel about yourself with their approval, admiration, and respect. The Ph.D. has not been acquired because it was not conceived from the truest part of you, neither was the Masters degree nor the business for that matter. You haven't failed to accomplish these goals, they just haven't come from the truest part of you and, as such, they haven't provided lasting inspiration.

When you are humble enough to collect the gifts of your past experiences, you are then able to begin an internal process of connecting with the self to truly know what you want out of this life. When people make choices based on factors external to the truest self, they have experiences of perceived failure if the outcome is different from what they expected. When you filter your perceived successes and failures through your truest self, perceived failures and successes serve as guidance to find or confirm your true gift, that unique light that only you can shine on this world.

Living in the moment allows you to show genuine emotion for everything. Happiness and a peaceful disposition will become your common state of being. You will express gratitude for your opportunities and the people in your life. You will be able to focus on the moment and experience the full range of emotions given to you. You'll be humbled by your successes and learn from your perceived failures. Most noticeably, when you are living in the moment, you release negativity easily and are contagiously optimistic. People living in the now have strong faith, profound hope, quiet charity, and, most importantly, they *live with integrity.*

**Nothing is at last sacred but the
integrity of your own mind.**

*Ralph Waldo Emerson,
"Self-Reliance"*

FOUR

Live With Integrity

So that you can be consistent and whole in all your experiences.

Many of us think of integrity as honesty. While honesty is a part of the definition, it is only a small part. Integrity is the transfer of our character, values, beliefs, and attitudes to all of our experiences.

What do you know about yourself? Do you change depending on your surroundings or are you consistent with your sense of self regardless of the circumstances? When your self is integrated, you are the same person whether in the role of father or employer; you are the same whether friend or doctor; you are the same whether homemaker or janitor. You are never defined by what you do; what you do is defined by you.

When you practice self-love, integrity is a character trait that is developed naturally. The essence of self-love is choosing to always be true to the self. If you are always true to self, then you are always true to others, and that's integrity.

Love is the glue that binds humanity together and integrity is the glue that binds you together. It is the fourth reminder and the mother of all virtues.

That's a powerful way to look at love. How does integrity do the same thing as love?

Love is the fundamental universal energy that is the omnipresent element of your existence. Everything else separates you from others, but love gives birth to your unity.

Look at hate, competition, success, religion, politics, and even spirituality. In this puzzle of a world people can't agree on a universal meaning for any of these concepts, but there is no questioning what love does—it unifies.

What love does for the universe, integrity does for the person. Not only does integrity ensure the oneness of your person, but it also brings courage and authenticity to your interactions with each other which creates a solid foundation from which to understand each other.

Because of integrity, you embody your beliefs, attitudes, and values across experiences so that you are consistent, wherever you are. The person who shows up to church is the same person who shows up at work, school, and play. The respect you give to your friends is the same respect you give to your foes. The roles you play do not define who you are; you define the roles you play.

> So even during adversity, competition, and conflict, integrity should be salient?

Especially during adversity, competition, and conflict. If you have self-love then you have love for others, especially during times of conflict. You may disagree or even stand opposed to others, but you disagree on specific points and stand opposed on specific issues as a person of love. You may believe you hate a person because of his or her choices, but it really doesn't mean you hate the entire person, just the choices the person has made. If those choices change favorably, so too will your feelings for the person, maybe not immediately but certainly over time. Self-love does not allow you to compromise others because to do so would be a compromise of the self.

> So, if I don't have self-love, it's not possible to have integrity?

You really have to go against your truest self to not have integrity. People who don't practice self-love unfortunately betray themselves often, without even knowing it. Self-love dictates honoring the self and honoring the self means honoring others.

> Probably the greatest challenge I am facing today is maintaining integrity. Perhaps this is not surprising since some of the greatest institutions and organizations

are affected by the lack of professional integrity in their leaders.

You make the distinction of professional integrity as if integrity can be modified, but it is not the case. Integrity simply is. Integrity cannot be dissected and there can be no distinction in integrity. It is your personal code of conduct regardless of where you are. You cannot have high or low integrity, professional or personal integrity; integrity is unflinching and unchanging.

You choose whether or not to be a person of integrity. When you find an organization of integrity, what you have found really is a group of individuals with integrity leading the organization. Each individual's integrity contributes to the collective integrity of the organization.

There can never be integrity in the business world, in the schools, in the home, in the church, or any place until there is integrity in the individuals constituting those groups. Personal dishonesty, self-deception, and self-betrayal always compromise the integrity of any system whether it be a government, a business, a school, a church, or a family.

Integrity is the mother of all virtues. What does that mean to me?

If you had no other virtue but integrity, you would live a life of truth. Humans are born with love and goodness.

Left to their own devices, and integrity, they would remain full of love and goodness. You are children of God. Regardless of your beliefs, God represents all that is good, true, and virtuous. As children of God, love is your inheritance. When you lose integrity, you lose everything.

Many people are confused about God but recognize a greater energy that binds them together. Love is also a greater energy that binds you together. It is no coincidence that the explanation of love looks like the explanation of God; God is love. God is often referred to as the universe, the source, the creator, the organizing intelligence, the higher power, or anything but God. It matters not what you call it; it is what it is.

Talking about God and doing God are two different experiences. It is easy to postulate about the magnificence and virtues of living a life exemplary to God, but very few actually live that way. Do God in your thoughts and deeds and save the talk for others—that's integrity.

If you want to know integrity, look to the messengers of God like Jesus Christ, Buddha, Muhammad, and modern-day saints like Mother Teresa, Gandhi, and Saint Francis of Assisi.

> Not all of us can or will live the lives of saints. Not all of us can or will be messengers of God. When the bar is raised that high, how can mere mortals like me ever reach it?

You have heard this before—it's not the destination, it's the journey that counts. Reaching the level of those who have gone before you is not important; learning from them as you would learn from anyone else helps you to navigate your world. You are not here to be Jesus; you are here to be you. Jesus has provided a blueprint for mankind to live righteously, but you have to build the house where your soul dwells. Only Jesus can do Jesus; you must do you. Which, by the way, makes you one of the saints.

What about religion and integrity?

Religion is not God. Spirituality is not God. They are the means of getting to God. Taking a walk through the woods in awe of its magnificence is also a way to get to God. You confuse the method with the purpose and the purpose with the reason.

The integrity of many religious leaders can be questioned. Like you, they are human and are susceptible to the traps and trappings of a temporal world. The idea of religion is good, a community of people seeking to live in the sprit of God, but the execution is often contaminated by the idiosyncrasies of the leader. Suffice it to say that if you can find a church organized in a way that eliminates your suspicions of its authenticity and is accepting of other religions and all its people, then you will find a place for great spiritual growth.

You have gone along with the temptations of the world and were blown in the direction of expediency. Your values didn't often drive decisions, material success did. Mother Teresa summed it up nicely when she modified the Paradoxical Commandments by Dr. Kent M. Keith to write:

The Final Analysis
People are often unreasonable, illogical, and self-centered;
Forgive them anyway.
If you are kind, people may accuse you of selfish, ulterior motives;
Be kind anyway.
If you are successful, you will win some false friends and some true enemies;
Succeed anyway.
If you are honest and frank, people may cheat you;
Be honest and frank anyway.
What you spend years building, someone could destroy overnight;
Build anyway.
If you find serenity and happiness, they may be jealous;
Be happy anyway.
The good you do today, people will often forget tomorrow;

Do good anyway.
Give the world the best you have, and it may never be enough;
Give the world the best you've got anyway.
You see, in the final analysis it is between you and God;
It was never between you and them.

Integrity is not about being good, it is about being real. Without integrity you become unpredictable to your friends, your colleagues, your children, your parents, and, most importantly, yourself. The most trustworthy people walking this earth are those who have a firm understanding and adherence to their values, and their guiding principles—whether it be the Ten Commandments or *Reminder To Self*. Without integrity you are susceptible to the elements that are designed to remove you from your purpose.

In dealing with people you teach them how to treat you. If you are full of integrity and filter outside influences through an established sense of self, you have respect, compassion, and patience for yourself, then that's how others will treat you. It's not just how others will treat you; it's about how you treat yourself. Integrity is your personal watchdog, partner, and motivator. In order to establish and fulfill goals, you need to have integrity. If you do not honor your commitments to the self, you cannot honor your commitments to others.

Integrity stabilizes you and makes your character predictable. When you are predicable with your integrity, you gain trust of self and trust of others. Trust of self builds confidence; confidence build courage; and courage is your transportation to greatness. From your greatness you will *live in abundance.*

**When we quit thinking
primarily about ourselves and
our own self-preservation,
we undergo a truly heroic
transformation of consciousness.**

Joseph Campbell

FIVE

Live In Abundance

*So that you can give freely
and receive freely.*

Life is energy and energy is constantly moving. Nature, in all its glory, is a system of symbiotic relationships with an exchange of resources among all of its parts. The process of life is one where we creatively express ourselves to each other and for each other. We gain strength from giving of ourselves, and we give strength by receiving others. Scarcity emerges when we prevent this energy from circulating.

When we think of abundance, we think of plenteous resources, but abundance in its pure state is giving and receiving in balance. Abundance is required for the flow of energy, for the flow of life.

The fifth reminder for living a fulfilled life is abundance. The principle of abundance determines the quality of success you experience. The energy of giving and receiving is transforming.

Much of the world today operates on a scarcity paradigm where you hoard your resources, not for the good of the many but for the pleasure of the few.

> When I look at the history of mankind, I don't think "the good of the many" ideology has worked.

It depends on what you are talking about. If you are talking about political ideologies, then you are correct. History has shown that we cannot stifle man's need to be fully expressed. If you look at communism, for example, you will see that most of the great communist nations have fallen and those that exist are being held together by force.

If you are talking about the idea of service, then mankind has only survived because of attention to the needs of the many. Having said that, two sensitive and divisive subjects for discussion are religion and politics. These areas exemplify scarcity versus abundance in their reasoning and resources. Man has a tendency to surrender his individuality to politics and religion, but the principles discussed refer to the individual. If you live by these eight reminders, then any organizations formed of these individuals will exemplify their inherent principles and values. Build the man righteously, and all that he creates will be righteous.

The state of abundance is the state of giving and receiving. It is the state of balance and the essence of service. Essentially, it is a state of allowing energy to move back and forth like night gives way to day and the sun shares time with the moon. The seasons split their blessings into four parts, knowing that every year they get their turn to spend time on earth. Abundance recognizes that our resources are more than sufficient for our coexistence and with faith and mindfulness we will have our needs met.

Giving time, money, and resources is easy for many, and it represents some people's interpretation of abundance. For the self to be fully expressed, it has to give. You have to create and you have to release. Energy accumulates in the individual, and we must find a way to release this energy. This process is the creative release. A volcano erupts violently when it accumulates and has held onto too much gas, so, too, will you erupt if you cannot constructively release your natural creative energy.

Love is an energy that is not only directed at the self; you also need to release the energy by loving and giving it to others. The more you give love, the more love you have to give, and the stronger it gets. That is what being in a state of abundance does; the more you give, the more you have to give.

You cannot be only in a state of giving, though; you must also be available to receive. Without self-love, you will find it difficult to receive. People are more comfortable with giving than receiving for many reasons, including the fact that society values giving more than it values receiving, but there has to be a balance. It is just as important to receive as it is to give. If there is no one there to receive, who will you give to? Have you ever given a gift to someone who refused it?

Yes. I felt rejected.

Many people feel rejected when the gift they give is refused. It is not just the gift that was refused; it is that the energy of giving had no place to go. Can you imagine what would happen to society if the many gifts that have come out of the creative minds of mankind were refused? There would be no progress. In addition, if you are not allowed to release yourself creatively, you will implode, collapse inwardly. Implosion shows up in the form of self-abuse, physical maladies, or autoimmune diseases, where your internal system attacks itself. Likewise, you can explode, that is, redirect that energy upon your external systems, relationships, and structures in the form of anger and abuse.

When you are in a state of receiving, you are in a state of allowing others to express themselves fully. Receiving is not about getting something, it is about understanding someone; it is about participating fully in the natural order. You breathe in oxygen that flows from plant life and, in exchange, you exhale carbon dioxide that the plants take in to process so that they can give you oxygen, so that you can give them carbon dioxide. Imagine what would happen if the trees refused your carbon dioxide; all plant and animal life would cease to exist. The reverse is also true. If you refused oxygen from plants, mankind would cease to exist. It's a wonderful and progressive cycle, giving and receiving.

Can someone give too much?

Yes. There are people who are martyrs. They give to a point of excess that jeopardizes their own being. This type of behavior demonstrates a lack of integrity and diminished self-love. Self-love requires that you remain healthy so that you give authentically.

When you fly on an airplane, flight attendants give the preflight instructions. They advise that in the case of an emergency and the oxygen masks deploy, you put your mask on first, then help the people around you. You can see the logic in this order of things; if there are noxious fumes that impair you, you won't be able to help anyone, but if you secure yourself first, you can help as many people as you can reach.

The same is true for people who give to get. When you give in order to get something in return, you try to manipulate the principles of abundance where we give and receive without conditions. Nature models abundance for you to see. Its vegetation and natural resources provide unending support for life and it requires nothing. Yet, it receives everything.

> I always thought that abundance meant that we have unlimited resources.

You are part of a vast universe with tremendous resources. The boundaries of all your resources are unknown but you can see land being used up, which means it is possible that some of your resources are finite. Mankind adapts and survives and it is in that regard that your resourcefulness is unlimited. If your resourcefulness is unlimited, you might very well have unlimited resources. If you don't force the hand of nature, you can be here for quite some time.

> What does forcing the hand of nature mean?

You need to be kind to Mother Earth. Conventional thinking says that you will destroy the earth, but you won't. In a universal context, the earth will adapt. In doing so it might create conditions that will be unbearable to the human body as we know it. Those conditions might not be able to sustain life.

Living abundantly means being responsible with your resources. Many take on the attitude that "there is always more where that came from." This attitude results in recklessness and wasted resources. Abundance is optimally using your resources for the progress and betterment of mankind. In other words, take as much as you need, but make sure you need it.

Look at food. There is enough food wasted around the world to eradicate hunger. If all of us used only what we needed, we would reduce waste. In doing so, we could redeploy significant resources to make fortunate the unfortunate. In this country, we pay farmers to destroy excess production. It is quite astonishing when you think about it.

All that is needed to live in abundance is to keep the mindset that there is enough to go around and come around again, if you don't interrupt the cycle.

Why does it seem so hard for some to accumulate, wealth in particular, yet it is so much easier for others?

Some people have a scarcity mentality! There are wealthy people with a scarcity mentality but they are not happy people. When you live in abundance, you accumulate and redistribute. Of course you can only accumulate and redistribute resources because you cannot hoard virtues. Instead, you naturally redistribute virtues or lose them. What you have on the inside is what is naturally given to others. You give what you have; you show what you know.

Charity is an essential part of the human experience, but service to others is the mode of commerce. You may give some services away, but you will have to exchange some services for money in order to provide the necessities of life. The more people you serve, the wealthier you become. If your work is connected to your purpose, then wealth is spiritual as well as financial. Living in abundance means you charge a fair price for your service and give at least ten percent away.

You, and everyone, are endowed with a talent or a special gift, a piece of the universal puzzle. That talent is essential to your existence and to the people who need it. These gifts are especially exemplified in professional people, but they are present on all levels, from the most popular celebrity to a little-known mother that sings a lullaby to soothe her infant child. You make the mistake of thinking that what you do for money must be connected to your purpose. People entertain, edify, assist, and provide comfort, all of which are essential experiences to the human existence.

In the world of trade, if people gave all their services away, they would not be able to take care of their own well-being. If they charged for everything they did, they would be hoarding and preventing the flow of energy.

Additionally, they would operate counter to the nature of mankind to give, to express the self. Philanthropic endeavors represent the need of those who are financially successful to give, to release a portion of their good fortune to the less fortunate and continue the natural flow of energy.

To live in abundance is to actively participate in the creative process, so that you may deliver yourself to mankind and have your gifts received by those who depend on them. Reciprocally, you must receive the gifts of mankind to make abundance flourish.

> I realize that I have lived with a scarcity mentality all my life. I never seem to have enough. If I can get something for nothing, I will take it. I have negotiated to the point of frustrating people; you name the scarcity and I have felt it. How can I transform my mentality to become a part of the exchange of energy?

Begin with gratitude and end with appreciation. Gratitude is one of those virtues that prepares the universe to receive you and all that you desire. Gratitude is thankfulness and appreciation for your blessings great and small. You have everything you need to be living; otherwise, you wouldn't be. However, you look past your good fortune, trying to find other fortunes. Take the time to appreciate what you have. Otherwise, you may achieve other good fortunes, but you will look past them as well. You will then find yourself in a state of lack because you are never satisfied with your success. Like children with their toys on Christmas morning, you open one gift and move to the next one, wondering if there are more, and when you get to the last one, you immediately make a request for next Christmas without fully enjoying this one. Bob Marley sang about your insatiable nature of scarcity in the song *Real Situation*; "Give them an inch they take a yard. Give them a yard, they take a mile."

Appreciation keeps you grateful for your blessings and the people who are essential to your good fortune. If you realize truly that people are placed in your life deliberately, you will view and treat them with reverence, a feeling of deep respect and devotion to their well-being. Not only are people placed in your life to help you, but you are also placed in their lives to help them. You often discard relationships as you discard things for which you no longer have a need. When you function from the steady place of self-love you will give the best of you and receive those placed before.

This utopian explanation is great but our cultures promote constant movement toward worthy goals.

There is nothing wrong with that; you make progress because you are inquisitive, ambitious, and persistent. Your world cannot be static but excess, however, creates lack.

As a society, we have become insatiable in our quest to accumulate things. There was a time when we were communal people and used only what we needed. Now, the more we get, the more we want. At that point, you are no longer working for survival or the enjoyment of life, you are working to accumulate. This insidious practice is hidden under the noble intent of security for the family and creating a legacy, while we reduce our resources and transform the living conditions for future generations. What good is having money without clean air and water?

Excess creates lack because the more you get, the more you want. Interestingly, if you are ever unfortunate enough to accumulate wealth so that your descendants have no need to work, pray that they find ways of constructively releasing their energy; otherwise they will become victims of your good fortune.

There have been a number of cases where children of the wealthy met with untimely deaths due to drug overdoses, car and airplane crashes, and suicides and homicides. These are all examples of excess in one area creating lack in another.

The process of life is the same for everyone, irrespective of socioeconomic position. You are here on this earth to experience the self as a unique part of an intricate system of life. You are your greatest contribution to this life. Connecting with the truest part of you ensures that you give the best self in the form of service.

An attitude of gratitude keeps the fortunate grounded and the unfortunate hopeful. This awareness creates an opportunity for energy to flow between the two, creating balance and the exchange of all types of energy. When you are aware that we live in a world of abundance, your fear of shortage is eradicated. You become more generous, both in shining your light and allowing others to shine theirs.

> How do I show gratitude, especially if I can't give money or otherwise?

Be thankful for everything. You always have something to give, even a smile. Allow people to give to you, even a smile.

Gratitude allows you to feel the joy and excitement that is alive in each moment. You are able to see and feel all the blessings around you and are not only willing, but also glad to share what you have been given. Being grateful for all that you have allows you to dream and let energy flow in, out, around, and through you so that you may become the light that God intended. It is up to you to feel and be this love, so that you may make deliberate choices full of integrity and truth, bringing about abundance in love, health, wealth, and meaningful relationships. In living your truth in your light, you must remember to *detach from your outcomes.*

Relinquish your attachment to the known, step into the unknown, and you will step into the field of all possibilities.

Deepak Chopra,
"The Law of Detachment"

SIX

Detach From Your Outcomes

*So that you can be courageous with
your choices and let your connection to
God manifest its miracles*

Everything happens in the fullness of its own time. You get to make the wish, but the universe determines when it comes to pass and exactly what it looks like. Rest assured though, it will come in some way, shape, or form. We tend to be consumed in the outcomes of things, which invariably removes us from our present moment and our responsibility for the experiences therein. One of our pure joys and blessings is our ability to create. In creating we find our challenges and in challenges we find life. We gain courage, understanding, knowledge, and wisdom. We see possibilities never before seen and meet a self we never knew existed. Our responsibility is to do everything we can, and then leave the rest to God and watch the miracles unfold.

Your reason for being here on earth is spiritual growth through temporal experiences of service to each other. From birth until death you will evolve through various stages of your human experience. To have the fullness of your time here on earth you must remember *to detach from your outcomes*. Your life is a journey not a destination.

> This means that as I make my way through life, I have to stop and smell the roses because that's living.

As you have been taught that's exactly right, but life *is* the smelling of roses while you are on your way to something else.

> What's the difference?

The difference is that the smelling of the roses is life, not the something else that you are on your way to. It is a result of living in the moment. If you are magnifying the moment, then there is nowhere else to be. Even if you are not enjoying the moment but you are deliberate with your choices in the moment, then there is nothing else to do. If you are actively expressing yourself or learning in a creative way that contributes to the well-being of self and others, then you are living in the moment.

> That sounds fine and dandy but the reality is that I don't always get to enjoy my moments and sometimes I have limited choices with little opportunity for creative expression.

It's natural for you, at some point or another, to have those feelings, especially when your freedom is threatened, restricted, or manipulated and your creativity is stifled. But, you have never been promised only pure joy. No one said life would always be easy. It is your idea of life and the reality of it that bring disappointment.

These reminders are not independent of each other; they are interdependent, much the same way everything else works in the world. By that I mean that they are mutually confirming, with overlapping experiences of each other. If you are in the moment, then by default you are detached from your many desired states of being and desired possessions; you are detached from the ways you think things should be. Detachment from your goals, dreams, and aspirations allow you to enjoy life in the present. Being present enables you to observe and adapt to the circumstances of your life as they unfold, learning and reforming beliefs to match the knowledge gained from the experiences of your moments. In doing so, you live a life free of anxiety and open to possibilities that exist in your vast universe. Living this way allows you to be at peace, a necessary condition for finding joy.

> I have heard this information before and I am confused about its meaning. Staying detached from your outcomes seems like a cavalier way of living. Based on what I know, greatness is never achieved by being cavalier.

You are right. Greatness is never achieved by being cavalier, but we are not talking about being cavalier. Detaching from your outcomes means that you have goals, dreams, desired outcomes in the first place. Desired outcomes are the way you think things could be and possibly should be. Men and women with visions of change have created the greatest of inventions and innovations because of having a goal or a dream. When you look at their journeys, though, where they ended up is very different from what they envisioned. When Thomas Edison invented the light bulb, he was not successful on the first try, nor did it end up looking anything like what he imagined. He had to release his many notions of what it should be until he had the divine inspiration to find what it was. When you detach from the way you think things ought to be, you create the space that allows God to assist you in your creations and in finding exactly how things will be.

You and your partners had the best intentions and a solid plan when you created your old company. You wanted to be a sizable organization that helped an underserved group of people and also secure your financial future. That didn't work. After almost nine years, you found yourself in a professional crisis that took the better part of a year to understand. In that year you were attached to what did not happen, what you called failure. When you finally got through it, you detached from it. In fact, you had to detach from it to get through the hurt, pain, and disappointment. Only after your detachment could you write and, accordingly, it is only because of your experience that you had the inclination, passion, and time to write. Here you are, greater than you have ever been, serving people as you desired, but much differently than you had planned.

> So when I am emotionally affected by my circumstances, I am attached to them, but when I am unaffected emotionally I am detached?

Not necessarily. You could be attached in both cases but in the case where your emotions are not impeding you and you find the gifts in your misfortunes, you have released your attachment to them. When you are attached and the vision doesn't manifest as predicted or hoped for, you must release it and move on.

> What is meant by "release and move on?"

Forgiveness.

Forgiveness is the ultimate form of detachment and a way of bringing completion to past events. You don't forgive for the benefit of others, you forgive for the benefit of yourself. When a driver cuts you off on the highway with his car, that aggression upsets you to the point that you would pursue him. By the time you realize what happened, the driver is long gone but you are left feeling angry and vengeful. When you forgive here, it's not for the other driver's benefit but for yours. When you forgive, you are able to stay present and, in this case, focus on the drive.

To forgive yourself and others is to release the emotional bondage to your experiences and move on to other possibilities that await your light. Forgiveness is the toll you pay to continue on your journey of life. It allows you to create space so that God can enter and align you with your place in the universe and its need for you.

If the consequences of your actions are not similar to your vision, find the gift imbedded in the undesired outcome and move on. In every mistake and misfortune there is a life lesson for you to learn. The lesson might be obvious and immediate or, in many cases, obscure and delayed. When your choices are deliberate, you are given divine guidance that often can be seen immediately. The mistakes you made running your business created the circumstances around your decision to leave. Your decision to leave created the opportunity for reflection and contemplation that, in turn, allowed you to pursue your dream of writing and speaking professionally.

In living deliberately you have dreams and goals to provide service to others that make their journeys easier. The world is filled with infinite possibilities. To have your dreams and goals manifest exactly as you see them requires an alignment with a specific possibility. Alignment of that precision is like finding a needle in a haystack. It is easier for you to be flexible than it is for the universe to reorganize itself to accommodate you. Just because you want to be President doesn't mean you are going to be. Flexibility allows for a shift in your perception so you can see your unique place in the infinite possibilities of your human existence.

> Isn't this a contradiction to what others have said about partnering with the universe to manifest my creations?

Knowledge often comes from contradictions but this truth doesn't contradict other ideas. You don't know yourself well enough to trust all that you think, so your life is a process of trials and errors, what works and what doesn't, what connects to the truest part of you and what does not. You may think you want material wealth, but wealth may not be the yearning of your spirit.

> I thought I wanted to develop and lead a corporation, but that did not give me the satisfaction I expected.

You are getting the picture. What you originally thought you wanted turned out not to be so, at least not during that time of your life. Being able to detach from your outcomes will bring you peace and opportunities to allow miracles to unfold in your life, but you must be open to the evolution of the self. Life is a dynamic experience. You may very well be suited to lead a corporation, but your timing could have been off. There must be alignment for you to experience contentment. Your constant connection to God and the universe is essential for the manifestation of miracles.

> Miracles are biblically trite and can be esoteric to the lay mind. The idea of a miracle also takes the responsibility from the individual and gives it to God.

You think that a miracle is an experience, event, or an achievement that defies the logical order of your linear thinking, but all of life is miraculous. You have taken your experiences for granted, so you don't see the ordinary miracles like a smile, sunshine, music, and sweet potato pie.

The miracle of Jesus feeding 5,000 people with a few fish and a few loaves of bread is only superseded by the people's ability to digest the food. Your tendency is to overlook the ordinary for the extraordinary, but when you shift your perception you will see that ordinary miracles are the fabric of your life. Miracles require your involvement. With detachment, you create all the conditions necessary for a miracle to occur, then move on while God does the rest.

> Being able to move on required me to detach from my "failures" and for the most part I have done that, but I still have some residual emotions of disappointment and even resentment.

You are still attached. You don't truly see the blessings of your past. Your feelings can determine how you live your life in the moments you are given. The feeling of resentment will be an impediment to your learning. If you are not focused on self-love, you will not be able to extract the blessings from your experiences. You will live a life of regret and resentment when you realize that the reality of life is different from your idea of what it should be. Life is a school where lessons for living are always being taught. Understanding this fact allows you to stand outside of your experiences and see the guidance you are given.

Everyone, at some point or another, is victimized by another. It is in man's nature. The only difference between those who accomplish great achievements and those who do not is that great achievers find the lessons in being victimized. In fact, they might tell you that they were not victimized at all. Instead, they have had some very difficult lessons from which to learn, and learn they did. Your curriculum of life is loaded with lessons for you. Until you stop being a victim and start being a student, you will be given many opportunities to gain mastery. Your experience may be horrific and your situation may be dire, but until you can liberate yourself from your perceived self, you will continue to be a victim of your circumstances. You can only be victimized if you accept being a victim.

Experience is the perfect teacher. Be the student to learn the lessons. When you are detached from the way things should be, you become open to the way things are, which is the only place from which you can create change.

> By this account, then, it is not possible to achieve much, let alone my greatness, if I don't detach from my outcomes and use the circumstances of my life as raw material from which to create?

Along the journey of your life you will experience great triumphs and great disappointments. You must be able to stand outside those experiences and observe their value to your purpose. To be able to see their value you must be able to detach from all of it. It is easier said than done, but the more you do it, the easier it gets.

Isn't this about faith, really?

It is exactly faith. Faith is trusting that if you do your part, God's part will be done. By yourself, one plus one equals two. With God, one plus one equals two thousand. This is the essence of detachment and the experience of miracles. You release who you think you are so you can find out who you really are. You release what you think you can do so you may find out what you can really do. You release the way you think things should be so you may find out what they really are. And, ultimately, you release what you think God is so that you may find out what God really is. As you release, you detach, and as you detach, you align yourself with God and all the miracles that are available to you to *open up your heart* and shine your unique light so that you may be a part of the puzzle that you are here to complete.

As far as we can discern,
the sole purpose of human existence
is to kindle a light in the darkness
of mere being.

Carl Jung, Memories, Dreams, Reflections

SEVEN

Open Up Your Heart

So that you can shine your unique light and be a part of the puzzle you are here to complete.

Debbie Ford tells a story about a teacher who, in preparation for her kindergarten class, purchased a puzzle with the exact number of pieces as students in her class. The teacher wrote the name of each student on the back of each puzzle piece and placed it on each child's desk. As she began her class she noticed an empty desk—a child was missing. This was a problem because the lesson that she wanted to teach was that the students are all individual pieces that make up the puzzle of her class. Intuitively she made the point that the students are all as unique as the pieces in a puzzle and when one is missing the puzzle is incomplete. That's the way life is; we need each other to complete this puzzle of our world and when one of us is missing, the world is incomplete. Each one of us is a resource for the next and each one is a teacher to the other.

Whether you are a carpenter, a doctor, a professor, a student, a homemaker, a singer, a dancer, or a garbage collector, each one of those roles is as critical as the next. We are equals in the eyes of God and must be equals in the eyes of each other.

OPEN UP YOUR HEART

You are all a part of a grand system; a divine manifestation of moving parts that are synchronized to execute the plan of the Creator. Every part is needed. If parts are misplaced, distressed, or missing, the system will not function efficiently and may eventually collapse. It is important that you open up your heart so that you can shine the unique light you have within.

> What does misplaced, distressed, or missing mean exactly?

Some people are not true to themselves. They play roles that are not filtered through the truest self but through the expectations of others. When you are not true to yourself, you are misplaced and wedged into place, which in reality is out of place. If you are out of place for too long, the parts of you that are wedged into place become distressed, like a bicycle wheel rubbing against its frame. Eventually it begins to disintegrate. While you are misplaced and distressed, you are absent from the true purpose of your soul's journey.

In this grand system that I liken to a puzzle, you are an individual piece, with your unique specialty, with your unique talent. Like a puzzle, you might be able to recognize the picture with a few missing parts, but the evidence of your incompletion is glaring.

When you don't show up with your unique gift to mankind, mankind is incomplete. Look at the world around you; you are not a complete puzzle. It is in a state of confusion and dysfunction. Jealousy, envy, competition, coercion, and scarcity create a state of disharmony where the best advice to the developing mind is to find someone to emulate and do what they have done. It doesn't work that way. If you do what they have done, you may get what they have got but that may not be the way to fulfill your purpose.

It sounds like an argument for destiny.

It's about having a predisposition to a thing, a way of being. It's an experience where you most feel alive, where all that you are is activated, where passion and satisfaction take a stroll though life. As for destiny, your destiny is whatever you decide it to be. As a man thinketh, so is he. "What the mind can conceive and believe, it can achieve," wrote Napoleon Hill.

You have free will. That means you can choose the way you align with your purpose. You have the responsibility of finding how to fulfill your purpose and vehemently pursuing it so that you can be a part of the puzzle you are here to complete. You may have to evolve through levels of development where your interests lead to skills that support a primary talent that releases a passion that connects you to the purpose of serving others. You are fully actualized when you are functioning from your truest self. Only then will you find inner peace.

> I have had inner peace in moments, short moments. I can't imagine what it would be like to have continual inner peace. I am searching for my purpose. I have been in sales, have been a real estate investor and an entrepreneur, but none of those things have satisfied me.

You do not have to search for your purpose. Your purpose is to serve others. Your talents determine how you serve. When you are true to yourself, you will discover your talents. Discovering how to use your talents to serve will help you to find inner peace.

When you have an integrated self, you are functioning from the truest self—mind, body, and soul in alignment. As mentioned earlier, when you are wedged into place, which is really out of place, you will eventually disintegrate. You will literally destroy the wholeness of yourself mentally, physically, and spiritually.

You have only named your occupational experiences as ways that you have attempted to connect to your purpose, but joy will be experienced temporarily and compartmentally if you are just concentrated on work and material wealth. Selling your talents alone will not provide joy. What about God, your family, your friends, your community, and your fellow man? These relationships must also be considered when finding inner peace. Service to others through your truest self is your purpose for being.

> Purpose is mentioned in every one of the reminders.

Life is not as complicated as it seems to be. You have often wondered about the meaning of life. You have thought about the purpose of life. Hopefully you have gathered by now, your purpose here on earth is to serve. As you express yourself through your talents and receive others as they express themselves through their talents, you are in service. Every moment in your life presents an opportunity to serve and be served. If a homeless soul on the street begs for a dollar, give it to him. If your daughter wants to wrestle with you, wrestle with her. If you are walking by a person with a frown on her face, smile at her. If someone smiles at you, smile back. If someone offers you help, let them help. Honor the spirit of those who give, they need you. Honor the spirit of those who receive, you need them. Treat those put in your path with reverence, they are your reason for being. There is one purpose with many ways.

When you know how you are to serve, you know the reason for which you exist. Certainty about your purpose in life allows you to be in the moment. As you are in the moment, you are nonjudgmental and open to the uncertainty of your experiences. As you live in the present you will be more enthusiastic in your day-to-day living. The more you are in the present and focused on your purpose, the more likely you will attract the attention of people to support you. The more people you attract, the more people you are able to serve and the more successful you will be. The more successful you are, the more certain you are about your purpose. The cycle creates a process that attracts to you the resources and circumstances you need to move the vision of what you want into a manifested reality.

I have heard that process called the law of attraction.

The law of attraction is a metaphysical principle that describes what happens if you are focused mentally, physically, and spiritually on a thing. When you are melded in mind, body, and soul with your sights set on a particular outcome, you see nothing else, you hear nothing else, and you surround yourself with nothing other than the resources that can help you bring your focus to fruition. Everyone has the ability to be brilliant. Everyone has the faculty to uncover brilliance. Everyone has the responsibility to shine. Nelson Mandela quoted Marianne Williamson from her book, *A Return To Love*, in his inaugural address when he became the President of South Africa:

> Our deepest fear is not that we are inadequate.
> Our deepest fear is that we are powerful
> beyond measure. It is our light, not our darkness that most frightens us. We ask ourselves,

who am I to be brilliant, gorgeous, talented, fabulous? Actually, who are you *not* to be? You are a child of God. Your playing small does not serve the world. There is nothing enlightened about shrinking so that other people won't feel insecure around you. We are all meant to shine, as children do. We were born to make manifest the glory of God that is within us. It's not just in some of us; it's in everyone. And as we let our own light shine, we unconsciously give other people permission to do the same. As we are liberated from our own fear, our presence automatically liberates others.

I have now realized that whatever I have done has always been determined by other people's perceptions of my proficiencies—my family, my teachers, my friends. I was in sales for the longest time because it came naturally to me, but it wasn't satisfying. Every leadership position I have held has been because I was thought to be a good leader, but I have always felt inadequate, and as a result haven't thought myself very good at performing these tasks.

No one can assign you a purpose; that part has been done. You may have varied experiences where you hone skills and uncover talents, but connecting purpose is an internal discovery. You must rely on your unique combination of talents, experiences, and deep desires to discover how you'll serve. The people in your life are a tremendous asset to you. They can often see you in ways you are unable to see yourself, but you must experience yourself to know yourself.

How can you know if you like papaya without tasting it? You can watch someone enjoy it, you can listen to someone describe it, you can even smell it, but to know if you like it, you have to taste it. Likewise, you have to experience the way you think you are to serve to know if it connects you to your purpose. Like you have done, many have confused skill with talent and talent with purpose.

Your skills and talents are tools for your purpose. A skill is usually gained through experience and training. A talent is a natural God-given ability to do something well, your unique light. Dr. Martin Luther King and Mahatma Gandhi were great orators who moved people at a deep level with the sounds of their voices, but oration was their talent not their purpose. Their purpose was to pursue equality for all—service. The skill of speech writing is necessary to compose a good speech, but a talented orator makes a good speech great.

A person will spend almost thirty years training to become a surgeon. The purpose of a surgeon is not surgery, but saving lives. That is a long time to prepare to serve, only to find out that you are not passionate about that way of serving. People are always wanting what they believe they cannot have—riches, fame, and beautiful things. These things are tools to help you get to your purpose. Your ultimate purpose is service to others from the truest part of you. Your talents and good fortunes determine the way you will serve. The recognition of talent and the accumulation of fortunes are of no use to you unless your talents can be expressed and your fortunes can be shared.

You may have many talents, but only those talents that satisfy your soul are in alignment with your purpose for being. To find your satisfaction, you must travel the journey of your life. The journey of your life has many paths you must walk to uncover your connection to your purpose. When the steps you take and the directions you follow are filtered through your truest self, you will be living your purpose.

Your friends, family, and teachers can objectively view your talents in ways unseen to you. In their service to you they will provide feedback and encouragement so you can maximize your gifts. Your responsibility is to filter this feedback through the truest part of you. A talent for singing doesn't always mean that you are to make a living singing. You get to decide whether you should play professional basketball if you have that talent. Others can identify and help to develop your talents, but you are responsible for how to use them.

> How do I know my connection to purpose?

If you cannot let go of the way you think you should be, regardless of circumstances, you are probably aware of your purpose. If the way you think you should be inspires you, you are probably aware of your purpose. If the way you think you should be ignites your passion and compassion, you are probably aware of your purpose. If, in spite of all your material successes and possessions, you are unfulfilled because of the way you think you should be, you are probably aware of your purpose. If the way you think you should be connects you to God, you are aware of your purpose.

When you find your connection to purpose, you allow others to find theirs. The world is in balance when you connect to another as you fulfill your purpose. Balance is true abundance.

> I am not sure I see the connection completely on how I allow people to find their connection to their purpose.

Who are your greatest teachers?

> Jesus, Buddha, Lao Tzu, Wayne Dyer, Debbie Ford, Napoleon Hill, Paulo Coelho, Dan Millman, Kahlil Gibran, Alan Cohen, Stephen Covey, Don Miguel Ruiz, my mother and grandmother are some of the teachers that have influenced how I think.

For you to shine your light, you have to be illuminated by the light of those who have gone before you. This is their service to you. This point is critical for you to understand; your position in the world is determined by everyone else's position in the world. The placement of every piece in a puzzle is determined by the placement of every other piece in that puzzle. Regardless of status and achievement, rank and placement, no piece of the puzzle is more important than any other piece. That is, none of you is any more important than any other of you. Society discriminates based upon material success, but in the eyes of God you are all equals.

When you are equals in the eyes of each other, your puzzled world is complete. How secure your place in the puzzle is is determined by how secure others feel in the puzzle. When you are your truest self, unique and secure in who you are, you allow others to be their truest selves, a unique and secure part of the puzzle of life. With this knowledge you now have a divine obligation to actively seek out that which serves your soul and the souls of others.

What is meant by a divine obligation?

You are expected to live deliberately, from your truest self. Pursue a way to serve others that brings you the most satisfaction. Every invention came out of service for others. Every creation was made to serve someone else. The most educated person is educated for service to others. There is not a person who is alive who doesn't serve someone. Service to others is your purpose for being. Without the opportunity to serve, you don't exist. Your divine obligation is your responsibility to self, God, and others. Taking full responsibility for finding your connection to purpose will allow you to experience the joy that this life has to offer.

Open your heart, be all you are. Give life to the parts of you that have been stifled, altered, hushed, disowned, and forgotten, in order to be accepted by those around you. Stop playing small to make others more comfortable. Live your truth; your world needs you to shine your light. Be that unique puzzle piece so that you and those who depend on you may *live today in joy,* your spiritual endowment.

**Once a man and twice a child.
And everything is just for a while.**

Bob Marley, Real Situation

EIGHT

Live Today In Joy

*As you've never lived a day, and
like you will never live another.*

Life is a gift and our greatest purpose is to experience the joy of it through service to others. That kind of joy comes only from being all you are. The only way to be who you are is through understanding and loving yourself completely, including your imperfections. As the love of self manifests, our choices become deliberate. When our choices are deliberate, we are living in the moment with integrity. Integrity is being your authentic self in all moments. When we are authentic, we live in abundance, optimally utilizing each other's talents and our natural resources on this adventure of life. As we give and express ourselves creatively while detaching from our outcomes, we open our hearts so that we can shine our light and realize how much we matter to this world. When we recognize how much we matter to the world, we recognize how much others matter to the world. With this awareness, our love for others flows freely in all directions. As our love for others flows freely, joy is created around us. When we are surrounded by joy, we are living in joy. When we live according to the precepts of these reminders, we live a full life.

Joy is the reward you reap for living a life filled with authenticity, truth, God, and the service of your fellow man.

> And when I find happiness, I find joy?

Close, but not exactly. Happiness is a necessary condition for joy, but not a sufficient one. If you are not in a state of happiness, you cannot experience joy. Joy is the place you go beyond happiness. You can seek happiness by creating conditions for it, but joy only comes when the stage of happiness has been set. Happiness is usually experienced when you accomplish something, when a desired outcome is achieved. Happiness is when you are on a much needed vacation that you've planned for, you've saved for, and you took time out of an active schedule for.

You find yourself in joy when, unexpectedly, a cool breeze blows in the hot sun while on this vacation and you realize there is nothing else you would rather be doing. Joy is experienced when you realize that right where you are is where you want to be. It is when you can see the perfection of all that is manifested in your moments, in your life.

> By this explanation I can find happiness and still not have joy?

Yes. Most of the time you are happy, but not joyous. Happiness is usually found in material things or temporal experiences. Joy is found in spiritual experiences. When your daughter stops you with no prompting and for no reason but to tell you that she loves you, that's joy; that's spiritual. A spiritual moment cannot be orchestrated. It is the synchrony of a mind-body-soul experience, activating the senses in such a way that results in a moment far greater than the individual experience of each or several of the senses combined could produce.

I am sure you have heard the phrase, "the whole is greater than the sum of its parts." That is the essence of a spiritual experience; that is the essence of joy. Look at the principles discussed. Individually they help you to live a life more fulfilling than you can without them, but collectively they help you to live an amazing life, a life in joy.

> The essence of joy is a spiritual experience and the eight reminders bring about conditions for that spiritual experience when they are experienced together?

Yes. Living this way is a process, not an event. Gandhi said that satisfaction is in the effort, not in the attainment. In smelling the roses you are passing along the way to somewhere else, you will find joy. Until you have the awareness that harmony of your mind, your body, and your soul is the one energy that connects to Source energy, you will dance in and out of your joy. Life becomes naturally more enjoyable as you spend longer periods in joy. In this life you get to work on it and these reminders are providence.

Everything starts with self-love. If you didn't have it before, you have it now. In quantum physics, it has been discovered that the moment you look at a thing you change it. Just being aware of self-love gives it to you. As you focus on it you will do more with it. That which you think about will expand.

With self-love you connect to your truest self, and if you have connected to your truest self, you have a conscious connection to God, your Source. God makes it all possible. Not only can you not have a conscious connection to God without self-love, but neither do you have a conscious connection to others. The relationship you have with God is the relationship you will have with others. The relationship you have with others is the relationship you will have with yourself because it's also the relationship you have with God.

There is a scripture that states, "Like a beggar comes unto us for money, we beg unto God for blessings and forgiveness. Should God respond to us the same way we respond to the beggar with judgment, condemnation, and rebuke? Or should we respond to the beggars as God responds to us with forgiveness, nonjudgment, and generosity?" You see, it's all tied together. How you respond to the beggar is how you respond to God, and how you respond to God is how you respond to yourself. How is that for a spiritual jolt?

When you become aware of the trinity of your divinity—you, God, and others—everything is a matter of choice or free will. When you choose deliberately, you become the author of your life's story. You decide if you will be your truest self. You decide how you want to be treated by others. You decide how you will treat others. You decide whether to walk with your Creator or to go it alone. Walking with your Creator doesn't necessarily mean that your journey gets easier, but you do get a constant companion. John Maxwell said, "One is too small a number for greatness."

> In any given moment I am many things to many people; I am a father, a husband, a neighbor, an entrepreneur, a writer, a speaker, a teacher, a student, a son. I am a promise to many.

You need to remind yourself of elementary truths. If you live with integrity, then you are your truest self in all your roles. You will give everything you can to do your very best without compromising yourself or others. Your outcomes will change depending on the health of your mind, body, and spirit, but because of your integrity you will be your best, regardless of your circumstances. You will be consistent and whole in all of your experiences.

You can't be Jesus; only Jesus can be Jesus. That puzzle piece is accounted for. He set the example for us to follow and left that blueprint for us to use as a guide. Jesus had a purpose and so do you. Sometimes you will fall away from your path. You will become the very things you despise, but in loving yourself it is possible to embrace all of that. You cannot constructively deny how you are, so embrace how you are and pursue how you would like to be. In embracing the qualities that please you and displease you, you are able to choose how to be from the desires of the truest self. When you give yourself that latitude, you can give others that latitude. Our brightest light is often found in our darkest moments.

These reminders are like simple virtues.

They are virtues and virtues are simple. You don't need to be a learned person to understand how to live joyously. You don't need to be financially wealthy to have access to these virtues. You don't need to be special in any way to have these virtues, but having these virtues makes you special in all ways, always. God is simple like that.

If you live any one of the reminders as your creed, you will naturally live all of them as your creed. You cannot be true to one reminder and violate the others. Conversely, you cannot violate one and be true to the others. Abundance is the manifestation of any and all of the reminders.

As you give and receive, you bring to life the exchange of your gifts and talents without an attachment to the outcomes of your actions. You allow the universe to sprinkle its magic over your piece of the puzzle so that you can produce everyday miracles, but you must show up ready to shine your unique light so that your world can be complete because you are in it. The universe absolutely needs you to be as special as you are without judgment or apology for your brilliance. Each one of us has the same amount of brilliance as the next, not by the opinions of man, but by the consecration of God. So go shine your light; plug into your Source; and experience the joy of being right where you are because you recognize your divinity and with it your ability to create a life of your own design; a life that magnifies your talents for the service to others.

**Look within, for within is
the wellspring of virtue,
which will not cease flowing,
if you cease not from digging.**

*Marcus Aurelius, The Meditations,
Book Seven*

The Beginning: Smelling Roses

Wisdom is the intersection of knowledge, life experience, introspection, and intuition. My experiences came to me at a gradual pace and then at the speed of life, which is somewhere between monotony and enlightenment. The speed of life varies, depending on the state of your mind, body, and soul.

The moment between what happens to you and how you respond to it determines the fullness of your life. In that moment you will experience instant and simultaneous stages of awareness, intuition, knowledge, and responsibility. What you do will result in the progression, regression, or stagnation of your truest self. Writing this book for me is an act of faith and a thousand steps toward my truest self.

You get to choose what to do with this information. Will you choose to welcome it into your life and experience the profound changes it will bring? Or will it end up on the shelf somewhere like everything else you have read or heard on living a fulfilled life? You have not been exposed to anything new here. Will this be a synchronistic moment when your desire for greatness meets the reminder of your greatness? Will you deliberately choose or will you continue to allow choices to be made for you? If you understand the first reminder of self-love, your choice has been simplified.

Beginning can be overwhelming and intimidating. We are often paralyzed by the magnitude of bridging the gap between where we are and where we would like to be. The trick is to see the picture and then lose the picture, referencing it only to see how your journey is progressing, how you are measuring up against it.

In other words, be in the moment. Only in this moment can you truly experience life. Only in this moment can you plan for your next moment. Only in this moment can you make course corrections. Only in your moments can you experience your love of self and therefore your connection to God. It is only in the moment that your truest self can be experienced.

The journey of a thousand miles starts with the first step. Here are your first three:

Step 1: Be Where You Are
Step 2: Know Where You Are
Step 3: Begin Where You Are

Be Where You Are: You are right where you need to be. All your choices have lead to this point and this point is where you have gained awareness of your importance. There is no need for unmanageable change without contemplation and understanding of your circumstances. Magnify your moment; make the very best of it. If you begin to invite your truest self into your life, your guidance is instant and your observation of your life will begin.

Know Where You Are: Through careful observation and contemplation of your life as it is, you will gain a better understanding of the role you're playing and the need for it. Your life is no accident. You are right where you need to be. Moving from where you are without proper understanding of your life will lead you back to where you are. The setting may be different but the lessons you need to learn will be the same. There is a reason for where you are and once you find it, you have choices to make.

Begin Where You Are: There is really no where else from which to begin. Once you gain perspective on your life, you get to choose how quickly you move. Most likely you will become better at what you are doing because you realize that where you are is one step—one necessary moment in your progression. In some cases you will move immediately because your truest self cannot come to life in your present circumstances. Either way, you now have an awareness of self and a need to be fully expressed, not from a place of lack, but from a place of liberation. Seek out the resources you need and the relationships that can help you. This is your time of movement; movement into where you are or movement out of it.

I would love to finish this book with a feel good epilogue. But I won't. I have gone through unimaginable changes in my life—in work, in play, and in family. Still, what seems to be my nadir is my summit. There are more mountains to climb and people to help climb. Along the climb, I look out on the open space and realize the magnificence of God. I know that a universal intelligence has guided me right where I need to be. As I stop to smell the roses I once passed, I realize that smelling the roses is why I am here.